Little Red Book
of
Synonyms

By the same author

Treasure Chest for Public Speaking
Read Write Right: Common Errors in English

Little Red Book Series

Little Red Book of SMS Slang-Chat Room Slang
Little Red Book of English Vocabulary
Little Red Book of Grammar Made Easy
Little Red Book of Euphemisms
Little Red Book of English Proverbs
Little Red Book of Acronyms and Abbreviations
Little Red Book of Modern Writing Skills
Little Red Book of Effective Speaking Skills
Little Red Book of Idioms and Phrases
Little Red Book of Antonyms
Little Red Book of Phrasal Verbs

A2Z Book Series

A2Z Quiz Book

A2Z Book of Word Origins

Others

The Book of Motivation
The Book of Virtues
The Book of Firsts and Lasts
The Book of Fun Facts
The Book of More Fun Facts

Little Red Book *of* Synonyms

Terry O'Brien

RUPA

Published by
Rupa Publications India Pvt. Ltd 2012
7/16, Ansari Road, Daryaganj
New Delhi 110002

Sales centres:
Allahabad Bengaluru Chennai
Hyderabad Jaipur Kathmandu
Kolkata Mumbai

Copyright © Terry O'Brien 2012

All rights reserved.
No part of this publication may be reproduced, transmitted,
or stored in a retrieval system, in any form or by any means,
electronic, mechanical, photocopying, recording or otherwise,
without the prior permission of the publisher.

ISBN: 978-81-291-1969-8

Third impression 2014

10 9 8 7 6 5 4 3

The moral right of the author has been asserted.

Typeset by Innovative Processors, New Delhi

Printed and bound in India by Repro Knowledgecast Limited, Thane

This book is sold subject to the condition that it shall not, by way of trade
or otherwise, be lent, resold, hired out, or otherwise circulated, without
the publisher's prior consent, in any form of binding or cover other than
that in which it is published.

*I dedicate this book to late Prof. A.P. O'Brien,
my father, friend, guide and mentor, who
inspired me to the canon of excellence:
re-imagining what's essential*

PREFACE

SYNONYMS: This term comes from Latin and from Greek *sunnumon,* from SYN + *onoma* name: "word having the same sense as another". In Linguistics, a synonym is a word that means the same or nearly the same as another word, such as *bucket* and *pail*. In Literary & Literary Critical Terms, it is a word or phrase used as another name for something, such as *Hellene* for a *Greek*. In Life Sciences & Allied Applications / Biology: *Biology* a taxonomic name that has been superseded or rejected.

In simple terms, it is a word having the same or nearly the same meaning as another word or other words in a language. It is a word or an expression that serves as a figurative or symbolic substitute for another.

Thus two words that can be interchanged in a context are said to be synonymous relative to that context equivalent word. A **thesaurus** is a reference work that lists words grouped together according to similarity of meaning (containing synonyms and sometimes antonyms) in contrast to a dictionary, which contains definitions and pronunciations.

Happy reading

Dr Terry O'Brien

Synonyms

A

Abandon vb.	Leave, relinquish, quit, forsake, desert, cede, give up,
Abbreviate vb.	Shorten, abridge, cut, condense
Abhor vb.	Hate, detest, loathe
Abnormal adj.	unusual, odd, peculiar, queer, strange, weird
Abolish vb.	nullify, put an end to
Abound vb.	teem, swell,
Abridge vb.	shorten, cut
Abrupt adj.	sudden, short, sudden
Abstain vb.	refrain, keep oneself from indulgence
Abundant adj.	plentiful, ample, replete, full
Accelerate vb.	hasten expedite, hurry, quicken
Access n.	approach, liberty to approach
Accompany vb.	escort, go with, join
Accomplish vb.	complete, achieve, realise
Accumulate vb.	pile, amass, gather, garner
Accurate adj.	exact, correct, precise
Achieve vb.	accomplish, perform
Acknowledge vb.	agree to, admit
Acquire vb.	obtain, procure, get, gain

Acquit vb.	forgive, exonerate, find not guilty
Active adj.	operative, engaged, busy
Actual adj.	real, true, genuine, certain
Acute adj.	serve, piercing, sharp, keen
Adage n.	proverb, saying maxim
Adapt vb.	conform, adjust, fit
Adjacent vb.	near, next(to), close, nearby
Adjourn vb.	suspended, postpone, put off, defer, delay
Adjust vb.	change, repair, fit, accommodate
Admirable adj.	excellent, worthy, praiseworthy
Admire vb.	esteem, like, find praiseworthy
Admonish vb.	rebuke, censure, reprove
Adoration n.	worship, reverence, homage
Adore vb.	worship, revere, venerate
Adorn vb.	embellish, decorate, beautify
Adroit adj.	skilful, adept, dexterous
Advantage n.	favour, vantage, edge
Adversary n.	opponent
Adversity n.	misfortune, distress, calamity
Advice n.	counsel, suggestion
Affirm vb.	declare, assert, say, confirm, ratify
Afflict vb.	grieve, distress, trouble
Affluent adj.	rich, wealthy, prosperous
Afraid adj.	frightened, scared, terrified
Aggravate vb.	intensify, make worse or more severe
Agony n.	pain, suffering

Agree vb.	concur, assent, consent, concede
Aid n.	assist, support
Ailing adj.	sick, ill sickly
Ailment n.	sickness, illness, disease
Alacrity n.	alertness, agility
Alarming adj.	shocking, appalling, daunting
Albeit adv.	Although, notwithstanding
Alias n.	pseudonym, pen name
Alien n.	foreigner, stranger, foreign
Alight vb.	disembark, debark, detrain, deplane, debus
Allegiance n.	loyalty, faithfulness
Alleviate vb.	relax, lighten, assuage, soothe
Allot vb.	distribute, divide
All-out adj.	complete, total, wholeheartedly
Allure vb.	entice, tempt, lure invite, attract
Ally n.	associate, friend, partner
Aloof adj.	distant
Alter vb.	change, modify
Altercation n.	argument, dispute, quarrel
Alternate vb.	interchange
Altitude n.	height, elevation
Altruism n.	devotion to others, love of others, philanthropy
Amass vb.	gather, accumulate, pile up, store up
Amateur n.	novice, nonprofessional
Amaze vb.	astonish, astound

Ambiguous adj.	unclear, uncertain, vague
Amble vb.	go at easy pace, dawdle
Amend vb.	improve
Amiable adj.	friendly, amicable
Amnesty n.	forgiveness, general pardon
Amorous adj.	loving, affectionate
Amorphous adj.	shapeless, formless, structureless
Ample adj.	plenty, spacious, abundant, plentiful
Analogous adj.	similar, resembling, alike
Anarchy n.	disorder, misrule, want of government, lawlessness
Ancestral adj.	inherited, hereditary
Anecdote n.	story, tale, narrative
Anger n.	wrath, fury, rage, **vb.** enrage, infuriate
Anguish n.	suffering, misery
Animosity n.	ill will, antagonism, hostility
Aphorism n.	maxim, proverb, saying
Apologetic adj.	regretful, sorry
Apology n.	explanation, plea, excuse
Appall vb.	horrify, shock
Apparel n.	clothing, clothes, garb, garments
Apparent adj.	plain, evident, clear, obvious
Appease vb.	pacify, calm, quiet, soothe
Append vb.	add, attach, supplement
Applaude vb.	praise, acclaim
Apposite adj.	apt, suitable, appropriate
Appraise vb.	evaluate, value, assay

Apprentice n.	learner, beginner, recruit
Apprise vb.	inform, acquaint, make aware, make known to
Appropriate adj.	fitting, proper, suitable
Approve vb.	endorse, confirm
Approximate adj.	nearly correct, almost exact
Apt adj.	proper, suitable, appropriate
Ardent adj.	fervent, eager, devoted
Arduous adj.	difficult, hard
Arid adj.	dry, dried up, unfertile, barren
Arouse vb.	awaken, stir, activate, stimulate
Artificial adj.	unnatural, man-made, not genuine, unreal
Ascend vb.	rise mount, go up ward
Ascertain vb.	determine, establish, fix, make sure
Ask vb.	question, inquire of, seek information
Aspect n.	point of view
Aspire vb.	yarn for, wish for, desire
Assail vb.	attack, assault, set upon
Assemble vb.	agree, consent, agreement, approval, permission
Assert vb.	declare, affirm, insist (on)
Assiduous adj.	industrious, diligent, active, untiring, persevering
Assist vb.	support
Assumption n.	supposition, presumption

14 Assure

Assure vb.	pledge, promise, guarantee
Astonish vb.	surprise, astound, startle
Astute adj.	shrewd, cunning
Atrocious adj.	awful, abominable
Attain vb.	accomplish, reach, achieve
Attire vb.	dress, cloth, apparel
Attractive adj.	appealing, alluring
Audacity n.	boldness, impudence, effrontery
Auspicious adj.	fortunate, lucky, favourable
Austere adj.	severe, harsh, firm, strict, stiff
Authentic adj.	genuine, real
Authority n.	jurisdiction, authorisation
Authorize vb.	empower, permit
Aversion n.	dislike, abhorrence
Avert vb.	ward off, avoid
Aware adj.	conscious, informed
Awe n.	respect, wonder, admiration
Awkward adj.	clumsy, sloppy
Axiom n.	truism, truth
Azure adj.	blue, sky-blue

B

Back vb.	support, assist
Backbite vb.	defame, malign
Baffle vb.	mustify, puzzle, confuse
Bait n.	lure, enticement

Ban vb.	forbid, prohibit **n.** prohibition
Banal adj.	trite, overused, hackneyed
Banish vb.	exile, deport, expel
Barren adj.	sterile, bare
Barricade n.	barrier, enclousure
Barter vb.	trade, exchange
Base adj.	low, immoral bad, evil
Bashful adj.	shy, timid
Basic adj.	essential, fundamental
Batter n.	flight, combat, war
Bawdy adj.	obscene, dirty, vulgar
Bear up vb.	endure, carry on, keep on
Beat vb.	strike, pound, batter
Beget vb.	generate, procreate
Begin vb.	start, commence, initiate
Blend vb.	intermix, mingle
Bliss n.	happiness, joy, rapture
Bloat vb.	swell, inflate, dilate
Block n.	impediment, hindrance, obstruct
Blue n.	azure, sapphire
Blur vb.	stain, **n.** smudge, smear, stain
Bondage n.	slavery, enslavement
Boom vb.	thunder, roar
Bore vb.	drill, hole, perforate
Bounce vb.	rebound, ricochet
Bounty n.	gift, generosity

Bourgeois n.	middle class, common, conventional
Bow vb.	stoop, bend, yield
Brawl n.	fight, melee
Brawny adj.	muscular, sinewy, athletic, powerful, robust
Breach n.	break, rift, violation, breaking
Break up vb.	separate, dismantle, take apart
Brevity n.	briefness, conciseness, terseness
Brief adj.	short, temporary, fleeting
Bring forth vb. phr.	exhibit, show, expose, make manifest
Bring up vb. phr.	rear, raise, nurture, educate
Brittle adj.	frail, fragile, breakable
Broad-minded adj.	open-minded, unprejudiced, liberal
Brood n.	litter, offspring
Brother n.	sibling
Bruise vb.	injure, hurt, wound, damage
Brusque adj.	curt, abrupt, blunt
Bulge n.	protrusion, bump
Bulk n.	volume, magnitude
Bulky adj.	large, big, unwieldy
Bureau n.	department, unit, board
Burly adj.	brawny, strapping
Byword n.	slogan, motto

C

Cabinet n.	council, committee, ministry, cupboard
Cacophony n.	discord, jarring, harsh sound
Cajole vb.	coax
Calamity n.	misfortune, distress, catastrophe
Calculate vb.	figure, reckon, compute, tally, measure
Calculating adj.	scheming, crafty, cunning, shrewd
Callous adj.	hardened, insensitive, apathetic
Calm adj.	quiet, peaceful, tranquil, mild, composed
Cancel vb.	delete, erase, set aside, recall
Candid adj.	frank, open, straightforward, unbiased
Cantankerous adj.	grumpy, irritable
Capable adj.	able, skilled
Capacity n.	volume, content, ability, capability
Capital n.	cash, money, assets, resources
Capricious adj.	fickle, inconstant, inconsistent, changeable
Capsize vb.	overturn
Captive n.	prisoner, convict, hostage
Carcass n.	body, corpse
Cardinal adj.	important, chief, principal, primary, prime, major
Career n.	profession, vocation, occupation, job

Caricature n.	parody, exaggeration, spoof, lampoon, burlesque, satire
Carnage n.	slaughter, massacre, genocide
Carve vb.	cut, chisel
Cascade n.	cataract, waterfall, fall
Cast vb.	throw, hurl, fling, toss
Casualty n.	victim, injure, wounded, fatality
Catalogue n.	list, inventory, record, directory, index
Catastrophe n.	disaster, accident
Catch vb.	seize, capture, take, grasp, grab
Category n.	classification, kind, type
Caution n.	vigilance, heed, warning
Cautious adj.	careful, watchful
Cease vb.	stop, end, put a stop
Celebrity n.	notable, dignitary, personage, hero, heroine
Celestial adj.	heavenly
Celibacy n.	abstinence from marriage, single life
Censure n.	disapproval, criticism, reproach **vb.** disapprove, criticise, condemn
Certain adj.	confident
Certainly adv.	surely, absolutely, definitely
Certify vb.	verify, validate, confirm
Cessation n.	stoppage, termination, finish
Chagrin n.	irritation, vexation, bother
Challenge n.	dare, threat, dare, threaten, defy
Chance n.	opportunity, **adj.** accidental, casual

Change vb.	exchange, substitute, replace modify, alter
Chant n.	song, singing, hymn, incantation
Chaos n.	disorder, confusion
Chaotic adj.	disordered
Characteristic adj.	typical, unique, exclusive **n.** character, feature, distinction
Charge vb.	price at, sell for, attack, assault, assail **n.** accusation, allegation
Chaste adj.	virtuous, pure, innocent
Chat vb.	talk, converse, talk
Cheap adj.	inexpensive, low-cost
Cheek n.	impudence, effrontery
Cheer n.	applause, encouragement, **vb.** gladden, encourage, applaud
Cherish vb.	nurture, treasure, hold dear, value
Chide vb.	scold, criticize, admonish, reprimand, rebuke, reprove
Chiefly adv.	mostly, mainly, principally
Chivalrous adj.	brave, valorous, noble, polite
Chivalry n.	nobility, gallantry
Choice n.	select
Choke vb.	strangle, throttle
Choose vb.	select, decide
Chop vb.	mince, cut, hew
Chore n.	task, work, duty
Chronic adj.	continuing, persistent, continuous, lingering perennial

Circuit n.	orbit, circle, revolution, course
Circumference n.	periphery, border, perimeter
Circumstances n.	situation
Cite vb.	quote, mention
Clairvoyant adj.	able to see without eyes, seeing by mesmeric influence, seeing trance
Clamour n.	din, noise, **vb.** demand noisily, shout
Clan n.	family, set, group
Clarify vb.	explain, clear, define
Clasp vb.	grasp, embrace, clutch, **n.** hook, catch buckle
Class n.	classification, grade, subdivision
Classic n.	masterpiece, first-rate work
Classification n.	category, order, class, arrangement, grouping
Clean adj.	neat, tidy, clear, dustless, immaculate, unsoiled, untainted, **vb.** dust, mop, scour, sweep, wipe, wash, rinse, cleanse, decontaminate, sterilize
Clear adj.	plain, understandable, lucid, **vb.** empty, acquit, emancipate, let go, remove
Clearly adv.	obviously, definitely, plainly
Clench vb.	set firmly, clasp firmly, grasp firmly, clutch, seize, hold
Clever adj.	bright, intelligent, shrewd, talented, gifted, smart, skilful, adroit, dexterous
Climate n.	atmosphere, ambience, aura
Climb vb.	scale, ascend, amount

Clinch vb.	grasp, grip, clutch, clench n. catch, grip, clutch, grasp
Cloak n.	cape, mantle, shawl, cover
Clod n.	lump, chunk
Clog vb.	congest, overfill, stop up, crowd, cram
Close vb.	shut, fasten, lock, include
Close adj.	near, nearby
Closet n.	wardrobe, cabinet, cupboard, locker
Cloth n.	material, fabric, textile
Clothe vb.	garments, clothing, dress, apparel
Cloud n.	haze, mist
Cloudy adj.	dim, obscure, vague, sunless, gloomy
Club n.	association, society, organisation
Clue n.	hint, suggestion
Clumsy adj.	awkward, ungraceful, unskilful, inept
Cluster n.	batch, bunch, clutch, vb. gather, assemble
Coarse adj.	rough, crude
Coax vb.	persuade, cajole, urge
Coerce vb.	compel, force, drive
Cogitate vb.	think, reflect, ponder, weigh
Coherent adj.	sensible, logical, rational
Coincide vb.	correspond
Coincidence n.	chance, accident
Coincidental adj.	chance, unpremeditated, unpredicted

Collateral n.	corroboratory, confirmatory, concurrent
Colleague n.	associate, collaborator
Collect vb.	gather, assemble
Colour n.	hue, shade, tone
Colourful adj.	vivid, impressive, striking
Colossal adj.	enormous, immense, gigantic
Combat vb.	fight, battle, n. fight, battle, contest, conflict, war
Combination n.	blending, mixture, composite
Combine vb.	blend, mix, unite, join
Come vb.	approach, advance near
Comfort vb.	soothe, relieve, console, ease n. solace, consolation, relaxation, ease
Comment n.	explanation, commentary, review, report, criticism, remark, observation vb. remark, explain, observe, opine
Commission n.	committee, board, vb. appoint, delegate, authorise, entrust, deputise
Commit vb.	entrust, delegate, empower, authorise
Commitment n.	pledge, promise
Commodity n.	goods, merchandise, article, wares
Communicative adj.	unrestrained, frank, unrestrictive, candid, open, straightforward
Compact adj.	compressed, packed
Companion n.	associate, comrade, mate, colleague, friend
Compassion n.	pity, sympathy, commiseration
Compassionate adj.	tender, sympathising, humane, kind

Compatible adj.	harmonious, agreeable
Compatriot n.	countryman, fellow-countryman
Compel vb.	force, coerce
Compensate vb.	repay, remunerate, recompense, reimburse
Compensation n.	pay, remittance, wage, salary, earnings
Compete vb.	contest, vie, rival, oppose
Competence n.	ability, skill
Competition n.	rivalry, contest
Competitor n.	contestant, rival
Compile vb.	collect together, combine, select and arrange
Complaint n.	objection, grievance
Complement vb.	supplement
Complete adj.	whole, full, entire, ended **vb.** finish, conclude, terminate
Completion n.	conclusion, end, termination, finale, finish, culmination
Complex adj.	complicated, intricate
Compliment n.	praise, honour, admiration **vb.** praise, honour, approve, commend
Complimentary adj.	free, free of charge, gratis
Comply with vb. phr.	Observe, yield to, consent to, assent to, accede to, agree to, conform to
Compose vb.	create, write
Composed adj.	relaxed, calm, cool, tranquil, quiet

Composition n.	easy, theme, paper, article
Compound adj.	mixture, aggregate
Comprehend vb.	understand, grasp, perceive
Comprehensive adj.	extensive, inclusive, broad, wide, complete, full
Compress vb.	squeeze, compact, press
Compromise n.	adjustment, settlement, mutual concession, **vb.** agree, adjust, settle
Compulsory adj.	unavoidable, obligatory
Compute vb.	calculate, reckon, determine, figure
Computation n.	calculation, score, tally
Comrade n.	companion, friend
Conceal vb.	hide, cover
Concede vb.	admit, allow, acknowledge, yield
Conceit n.	vanity, egotism, self-esteem
Conceited adj.	vain, arrogant, proud, egotistical
Conceive vb.	create, invent, imagine
Concentrate vb.	focus, ponder, centre, meditate, scrutinize
Concept n.	idea, thought
Concern vb.	interest, relate to
Concerning prep.	about, regarding
Concerted adj.	joint, united, combined
Concise adj.	brief, short, summary, terse, compact, condense, compressed, comprehensive
Conclude vb.	finish, end, complete, understand, deduce
Concoct vb.	devise, plan, contrive, design, frame

Concrete adj.	firm, definite, solid, specific
Condemn vb.	denounce, rebuke, blame
Condense vb.	reduce, abbreviate, shorten, abridge, diminish
Condition n.	state, position, situation, requirement, **vb.** train
Condone vb.	pardon, forgive
Conduct n.	behaviour, manners, deportment, actions, **vb.** behave, act
Confer vb.	award, bestow, grant
Confess vb.	admit, acknowledge, grant, concede
Confidence n.	trust, faith
Confident adj.	sure, certain, self assure, self reliant
Confine vb.	limit, restrict, hinder
Confirm vb.	assure, verify, corroborate, substantiate, validate, approve, ratify
Confiscate vb.	take, seize, appropriate
Conflict vb.	clash, contend, **n.** fight, battle, struggle, encounter
Confluence n.	meeting, junction, union
Conform vb.	comply, agree, correspond
Conformity n.	agreement, congruence
Confound vb.	perplex, puzzle, baffle
Confuse vb.	perplex, bewilder, mislead, mix up
Confusion n.	perplexity, bewilderment, uncertainty
Congregate vb.	meet, gather, convene
Congruity n.	agreement, congruence, accord
Connect vb.	unite, join

Connection

Connection n.	junction, union, link, bond
Conquer vb.	succeed, win, gain, achieve, overcome, subdue
Conscientious adj.	honest, upright, scrupulous
Conscious adj.	aware, awake, international
Consensus vb.	agreement, concord
Consent vb.	agree, permit, allow, assent n. permission, agreement, assent
Consequence n.	result, effect, issue
Conservative adj.	right-wing, conventional, moderate
Conserve vb.	preserve, keep, retain
Consider vb.	deliberate, reflect on, think of, regard, look upon, judge, estimate
Considerable adj.	quite a lot, a great deal, important, significant
Considerate adj.	thoughtful, polite
Consideration n.	attention, thought, reflection
Consistent adj.	agreeing, compatible, harmonious
Consolation n.	solace, comfort, sympathy
Console vb.	solace, comfort, sympathise with
Conspire vb.	plot, plan, scheme, intrigue
Constant adj.	unchanging, fixed, stable
Constitute vb.	make up, compose, form
Constitution n.	code, law
Construct vb.	build, erect, raise
Construction n.	building, raising, fabricating

Constructive adj.	helpful, valuable
Construe vb.	interpret, explain, expound, translate
Consult vb.	confer, discuss, deliberate
Consume vb.	use, use up, expend, eat, devour, destroy, devastate
Consumer n.	buyer, user, purchaser
Contact n.	meeting, touch, tangency, junction
Contain vb.	hold, be composed of, include
Contaminate vb.	pollute, soil, dirty
Contemplate vb.	think about, consider, study, deliberate on or over, reflect upon
Contemplative adj.	thoughtful, meditative, pensive
Contempt n.	scorn, disdain, malice
Contemptible adj.	low, base, mean, detestable, miserable
Contemptuous adj.	scornful, disdainful, insolent
Contend vb.	dispute, contest
Content adj.	happy, satisfied, pleased, contented
Contest n.	competition, match **vb.** dispute, oppose
Contingency n.	possibility
Continual adj.	regular, consecutive, connected
Continue vb.	persist, proceed, endure
Continuous adj.	uninterrupted, incessant
Contraband adj.	prohibited, illegal, unlawful, illicit
Contract n.	agreement, bargain, pact, treaty **vb.** agree, diminish

Contradictory adj.	paradoxical, inconsistent, opposing
Contrast n.	difference **vb.** distinguish, differentiate, contradict, differ
Contribute vb.	donate, give, bestow, grant, offer
Contribution n.	donation, gift, grant, offering
Contrive vb.	invent, make, manage, arrange
Control vb.	rule, dominate, command, crub
Controversy n.	dispute, argument
Convenience n.	accessibility, assistance, service, benefit
Convenient adj.	nearby, available, ready
Convention n.	conference, meeting, assembly
Conventional adj.	common, usual, regular, habitual, accustomed, routine
Conversation n.	talk, discussion
Converse vb.	talk, chat, discuss, speak
Conversion n.	change, alteration, modification
Convert vb.	change, transform, turn
Convey vb.	bear, carry, communicate
Conviction n.	belief, opinion
Convince vb.	persuade, induce
Cooperate vb.	unite, combine, contribute
Coordinate vb.	harmonize, adapt, balance, match
Copious adj.	plentiful, abundant
Cordial adj.	friendly, polite, genial, affable, warmhearted
Core n.	centre, heart, kernel

Corporation n.	company, business, conglomerate
Corpse n.	body, cadaver, remains, carcass
Correct adj.	accurate, right, precise **vb.** right, rectify, amend, admonish
Corridor n.	passage, passageway, foyer, lobby
Corrode vb.	eat away, erode, wear away
Corrupt adj.	dishonest, untrustworthy, crooked, perverted
Cost n.	price, value charge
Costly adj.	expensive, dear, high-priced
Costume n.	clothing, dress, clothes, grab, apparel
Couch n.	sofa, settee
Council n.	committee, board, cabinet
Counsel n.	advice, guidance **vb.** advise, guide
Count vb.	enumerate, total, compute, tally **n.** sum, total, number
Countenance n.	face, visage, appearance **vb.** approve, support, favour, encourage, assist
Counteract vb.	offset, thwart, counterbalance
Counterfeit adj.	fake, false, fraudulent, spurious, false **n.** forgery, imitation **vb.** forge, fake, falsify, imitate
Country n.	nation, state, land, forest
Courageous adj.	brave, fearless, dauntless
Course n.	advance, progress, passage, direction, way
Courteous adj.	polite, graciousness, respect
Cover vb.	spread, conceal
Covert adj.	hidden, concealed

Covetous adj.	greedy, avaricious
Cowardly adj.	afraid, fearful, timid, timorous, faint-hearted
Coy adj.	bashful, shy
Crack vb.	snap, split **n.** flaw, split, fissure, snap
Cracker n.	biscuit, wafer
Craft n.	skill, ability, talent
Crafty adj.	cunning, clever, shrewd, skillful
Crave vb.	desire, yarn for, want, long for, hunger for
Crawl vb.	creep
Crazy adj.	mad, insane, lunatic
Creak vb.	squeak
Create vb.	originate, invent, make, form, construct, design
Creative adj.	inventive, imaginative, original, ingenious, innovative
Credible adj.	believable, conceivable
Creditable adj.	praiseworthy, worthy
Creed n.	belief, credo, doctrine, faith
Crime n.	wrongdoing, misconduct, offense, infraction, violation, misdemeanour, felony
Criminal adj.	illegal, unlawful, felonious **n.** crook
Cringe vb.	wince, quail, flinch, tremble
Cripple vb.	maim, injure
Crisis n.	emergency, climax

Criterion n.	standard, test, touchstone, measure, rule
Critic n.	judge, reviewer, commentator
Critical adj.	faultfinding, carping, condemning, reproachful, disapproving
Crooked adj.	bent, twisted, curved, hooked, dishonest, criminal, corrupt
Crop vb.	harvest, produce, yield **vb.** cut, mop, mow, clip
Cross vb.	traverse, mingle, oppose **adj.** irritable
Crown n.	circlet, coronet, tiara
Crude adj.	rude, raw, coarse, unpolished, unrefined
Cruel adj.	heartless, mean, unmerciful, ruthless, brutal
Crush vb.	break, smash, crash
Cryptic adj.	enigmatic, obscure, vague, unclear
Culpable adj.	blameworthy, to blame, guilty
Cultivate vb.	till, plant, seed, harvest, educate, refine, teach, nurture
Cultural adj.	educational, instructive, elevating
Culture n.	refinement, breeding, cultivation, upbringing
Cumbersome adj.	awkward, unmanageable
Cunning adj.	clever, tricky, wily, crafty **n.** skill, ability, craft, wiliness, shrewdness

Curb n.	check, restraint, control **vb.** check, restrain, control
Cure n.	remedy, treatment **vb.** heal, remedy
Curious adj.	inquiring, inquisitive, praying
Current adj.	present, up-to-date
Cursory adj.	hasty, superficial, passing
Curt adj.	abrupt, short, brief
Curtail vb.	shorten, abridge
Curtain n.	shade, blind
Custodian n.	keeper, caretaker, guardian, protector
Custom n.	habit, practice, rule
Cutting adj.	caustic, bitter, scathing, acerbic, stern

D

Dabble vb.	work superficially, make slight efforts
Dainty adj.	delicate, petite, graceful, elegant
Damage n.	impairment, injury **vb.** impair, injure, harm, mar
Damp adj.	moist, humid **n.** moisture, dampness
Dampen vb.	moisten, slow, retard, inhibit
Danger n.	peril, risk, hazard
Dangerous adj.	perilous
Dare vb.	risk, challenge, defy
Dapper adj.	active, lively, brisk, agile, nimble
Daring adj.	courageous, bold **n.** bravery, courage, valour

Dark adj.	shadowy, murky, gloomy, dim, dusky, dismal, sad, gloomy, unhappy
Dashing adj.	flamboyant, impressive, handsome
Data n.	information, facts, statistics
Dauntless adj.	brave, fearless, bold, intrepid
Daydream vb.	muse, woolgather
Daze vb.	stun, confuse, perplex **n.** stupor, confusion
Deadlock n.	stalemate, still, impasse
Deadly adj.	fatal, lethal, mortal, baleful, deathly
Deal vb.	trade, do business, buy and/or sell, bargain
Dear adj.	loved, beloved, darling, expensive, costly, high-priced
Death n.	demise, decease
Debate vb.	argue, discuss **n.** discussion, dispute, argument, controversy
Debilitate vb.	weaken, exhaust
Debonair adj.	unbane, sophisticated, refined, well bred, elegant, dapper
Debris n.	wreckage, ruins, trash, rubbish
Deceit n.	deception, fraud, guile, deceitfulness
Deceitful adj.	insincere, fraudulent, deceptive
Deceive vb.	mislead, cheat, swindle, defraud, hoodwink
Deceptive adj.	deceiving, false, deceitful dishonest
Decide vb.	determine, resolve
Decipher vb.	interpret, unravel, unfold, reveal

Decision n.	determination, resolution
Decisive adj.	resolute, determined, decided, firm
Declare vb.	state, proclaim, affirm, assert
Decline vb.	deteriorate, diminish, lessening, incline, slope
Decompose vb.	rot, decay
Decorate vb.	enhance, furnish, furbish
Decoration n.	ornamentation, adornment, medal, citation, award
Decrease vb.	diminish, dwindle n. lessening, diminution
Decree n.	edict, order vb. order, declare, announce
Decrepit adj.	feeble, weak, enfeebled, dilapidated
Dedicate vb.	consecrate, sanctify, hallow, assign
Deduce vb.	derive, conclude, infer, draw as implication
Deduct vb.	subtract
Deed n.	act, action, achievement, feat
Deem vb.	judge, determine, regard, consider, hold
Deep adj.	low, bottomless, absorbed n. ocean, sea
Default n.	omission, defect, deficiency
Defeat vb.	overcome, vanquish, suppress thwart
Defect n.	flaw, weakness, blemish vb. desert, abandon, leave, forsake
Defend vb.	protect, guard, shield, uphold

Defence n.	protection, resistance, trench, fortification, barricade, rampart, fortress
Defer vb.	delay, put off, postpone
Defiant adj.	obstinate, rebellious
Deficient adj.	insufficient, scant, incomplete
Defile vb.	corrupt, pollute, debase
Define vb.	explain, designate, distinguish
Definite adj.	certain, clear, distinct, obvious
Definitely adj.	positively, assuredly, absolutely
Definition n.	sense, explanation, interpretation
Deft adj.	adept, clever, adroit, skilled
Defunct adj.	dead, expired
Dejected adj.	depressed, disheartened, discouraged, downhearted
Delay vb.	defer n. postponement, slowdown
Delegate n.	representative, envoy vb. appoint, deputize
Delete vb.	cancel, erase, remove
Deliberate adj.	international, planned, calculated, premeditated vb. weight, judge, reflect
Delicate adj.	dainty, fine, fragile, frail, weak, sensitive, critical
Delicious adj.	savoury, delectable, appetizing, luscious
Delight n.	pleasure, joy, enjoyment
Delightful adj.	charming, pleasing, refreshing
Delineate vb.	design, sketch, figure, draw
Deliver vb.	transport, give, offer

Deliverance n.	release, liberation, emancipation, extrication
Delude vb.	deceive, beguile, dupe
Deluge n.	flood, overflow
Delusion n.	fantasy, illusion, phantasm
Demand vb.	request, call for, claim **n.** request, claim, requirement
Demented adj.	mad, insane, crazy, mental, lunatic, psychotic
Demolish vb.	destroy, ruin, raze
Demonstrate vb.	show, exhibit, illustrate
Demure adj.	modest, shy, meek, bashful, coy
Den n.	lair, cave, cavern
Denial n.	refusal, rejection, proscription, prohibition
Dense adj.	thick, solid, packed, compact, crowded
Deny vb.	contradict, confute, repudiate, dispute, reject
Depart vb.	leave, go
Depend vb.	to rely on, trust in
Deplete vb.	exhaust, drain, reduce, empty
Deposit vb.	save, bank, store **n.** sediment, lees, dregs, addition, entry
Depraved adj.	corrupted, corrupt, vicious, perverted
Deprecate vb.	belittle, depreciate, minimize, disparage
Depress vb.	dishearten, discourage, dampen

Depression n.	cavity, dent, despair, gloom, melancholy, sorrow, sadness, hopelessness
Deprive vb.	deny, strip, bereave
Depth n.	deepness, profundity
Deputy n.	assistant, aide, delegate
Deranged adj.	mad, insane, demented, lunatic, crazy, daft, psychotic
Derelict adj.	dilapidated, decrepit, neglect, shabby **n.** tramp, vagabond, beggar
Deride vb.	ridicule, mock, satirise, lampoon, jeer, taunt
Derive vb.	receive, obtain, acquire
Descend vb.	move lower, climb down
Descendant n.	progeny, child, offspring, issue
Describe vb.	portray, characterise
Description n.	account, narration
Deserted adj.	forsaken, abandoned, relinquished, given up, lonely
Deserter n.	fugitive, runaway, defector, renegade
Deserve vb.	earn, merit
Design vb.	plain, intend **n.** pattern, plan, blueprint, sketch
Designate vb.	denote, specify, assign
Desirable adj.	wanted, after, sought-after
Desire vb.	crave, long for
Desist vb.	stop

Desolate adj.	deserted, lonely
Despair n.	hopelessness, desperation, discouragement
Desperate adj.	despairing, hopeless, reckless
Despicable adj.	mean, base, low, worthless
Despise vb.	scorn, dislike, disdain, hold in contempt
Despite prep.	notwithstanding, regardless of, in spite of
Despot n.	autocrat, dictator, tyrant
Destiny n.	fate, fortune, lot
Destroy vb.	ruin, demolish, raze, waste
Destruction n.	devastation
Detach vb.	separate, disengage, divide
Detain vb.	delay, restrain, holdback
Detect vb.	ascertain, learn, find out
Deter vb.	restrain, hinder, prevent, hold back, dissuade
Deteriorate vb.	degenerate, degrade, debase, vitiate
Determine vb.	decide
Detest vb.	despise, hate, loathe
Detriment n.	harm, damage, injury
Develop vb.	grow, expand, enlarge, advance
Deviate vb.	digress from, alter one's course, diverge from
Device n.	machine, tool, utensil, instrument, gadget, contrivance, plan, design

Devise vb.	invert, create, originate
Devoid adj.	empty, bare, void
Devote vb.	apply, dedicate
Devotion n.	adherence, love, loyalty, regard
Devour vb.	gorge, gulp
Devout adj.	religious, pious, devoted
Dexterous adj.	adroit, deft, skilled, skilful, proficient
Dialogue n.	conversation, discussion, exchange
Dictate vb.	deliver, record, order, command, direct
Director n.	tyrant, despot
Die vb.	decease, perish, expire, pass away, fade, wither, wane
Differ vb.	disagree, be at variance
Difference n.	disagreement, inequality
Differentiate vb.	distinguish, separate
Difficult adj.	intricate, complicated, obscure
Difficulty n.	hardship, trouble, predicament
Diffident adj.	bashful, shy, demure, coy
Diffuse adj.	dispersed, sparse, thin
Digest vb.	eat, consume, consider, reflect **n.** abridgement, abstract, synopsis, précis
Dignified adj.	serious, stately
Dignify vb.	elevate, honour
Dignity n.	distinction, stateliness
Dilapidated adj.	decayed, decadent

Dim adj.	shadowy, vague **vb.** obscure, dull, darken
Dimension n.	measure, size
Diminish vb.	lessen, shrink, reduce, wane
Diminutive adj.	little, small, minute
Dine vb.	feast, lunch, sup
Dip vb.	plunge, immerse, submerge **n.** plunge
Dire adj.	awful, horrendous, horrifying
Direct vb.	control, regulate, indicate, guide **adj.** straight, straightforward, frank, sincere, earnest
Direction n.	way, route
Directly adv.	straight, immediately, at once
Dirt n.	soil, filth, pollution
Dirty adj.	soiled, unclean, filthy, polluted
Disability n.	incapacity, injury
Disable vb.	cripple, incapacitate, weaken
Disadvantage n.	inconvenience, drawback, handicap, hindrance, obstacle
Disappear vb.	vanish
Disappointment n.	dissatisfaction, failure
Disaster n.	calamity, misfortune, accident, catastrophe
Disbelief n.	incredulity, skepticism
Discern vb.	distinguish, recognize, differentiate, perceive
Discerning adj.	judicious, acute, sharp, piercing

Discernment n.	perception, acuity
Discharge vb.	relieve, unloaded
Disciple n.	follower, supporter, pupil
Disciple n.	training, practice, exercise **vb.** train, control, teach, chastise
Disclaim vb.	disown, renounce, repudiate
Disclose vb.	reveal, show, expose
Discomfit vb.	confuse, perplex, baffle, ruffle
Discomfort n.	anxiety, malaise, uneasiness
Disconcerted adj.	agitated, uncomfortable, upset
Disconnect vb.	separate, divide, unhook, disengage
Disconsolate adj.	sad, dejected, morose, wretched, depressed, melancholy
Discontent adj.	displeased, dissatisfied, vexed
Discontinue vb.	cease, stop, interrupt
Discord n.	conflict, disagreement
Discount n.	deduction, reduction, abatement, rebate
Discourse n.	dissertation, treatise, sermon, address, converse, oral **vb.** speak, expatiate, confer
Discourage vb.	dispirit, dishearten, depress
Discover vb.	find, learn, find out, ascertain
Discreet adj.	tactful, judicious, prudent, wise
Discrimination n.	prejudice, bias, intolerance
Discuss vb.	talk about, deliberate, consider
Discussion n.	talk, conversation, dialogue

Disdain

Disdain vb.	scorn, contempt
Disdainful adj.	scornful, contemptuous, haughty, arrogant
Disease n.	sickness, affliction, ailment, disorder, malady
Disentangle vb.	unwind, unknot, untie, untangle
Disgrace n.	shame, dishonour, embarrassment
Disguise vb.	hide, conceal, camouflage n. mask, coverup
Disgust vb.	offend, revolt, repulse n. distaste, nausea, aversion, revulsion
Disgusting adj.	revolting, repulsive, nauseous, nauseating, repugnant
Dishonest adj.	corrupt, false, thievish
Dishonour n.	shame, disgrace, indignity, defamation
Disinterested adj.	neutral, impartial, unbiased, unprejudiced
Dismay vb.	scare, frighten, alarm n. fear, horror
Dismiss vb.	discharge, release, liberate
Disorder n.	confusion, turmoil, tumult, chaos
Disown vb.	repudiate, renounce, forsake, disinherit
Disparaging adj.	discrediting, deprecating, denigrating, defamatory
Disparity n.	inequality, disproportion, difference
Dispassionate adj.	cool, composed, unemotional, controlled

Dispatch vb.	send off or away, achieve, finish **n.** message, report, communication
Dispense vb.	distribute, give out
Disperse vb.	scatter, spread
Dispirited adj.	dejected, downhearted, disheartened
Displace vb.	move, dislocate, dislodge
Display vb.	exhibit, show **n.** showing, exhibition
Dispose vb.	arrange, settle, adjust
Disposition n.	nature, character, temperament, personality
Dispossess vb.	evict, dislodge, eject oust
Disprove vb.	invalidate, refute, controvert, deny
Dispute vb.	argue, debate, oppose, deny **n.** argument, debate
Disregard vb.	ignore, overlook **n.** inattention, neglect, oversight
Disrepair n.	ruin, decay, destruction
Disreputable adj.	dishonourable, disgraced, notorious
Disrespectful adj.	rude, impudent, fresh, impertinent, cheeky
Disseminate vb.	spread, broadcast, promulgate
Dissent n.	disagreement
Dissertation n.	treatise, thesis, disquisition
Distant vb.	remote, far, afar, away, separated
Distasteful adj.	disagreeable, objectionable
Distend vb.	dilate, swell, stretch
Distil vb.	extract by evaporation, extract by heat

Distinct adj.	clear, definite, obvious, plain
Distinction n.	honour, renown, fame, repute, prominence
Distinguish vb.	separate, differentiate, discern
Distinguished adj.	renowned, famous, honoured, illustrious, noted
Distort vb.	twist, deform, prevent
Distract vb.	divert, confuse
Distraction n.	diversion, confusion
Distress n.	anguish, anxiety **vb.** worry, grieve
Distribute vb.	share, deal, dole, mete out, allocate
District n.	region, area, section
Distrust vb.	suspect, doubt, mistrust **n.** suspicion, doubt, mistrust
Disturb vb.	annoy, bother, vex
Disturbance n.	commotion, disorder, confusion
Diversify vb.	alter, modify, change
Divert vb.	turn aside or away, deflect, amuse, distract
Divide vb.	separate, split
Division n.	separation, partition, segment, portion
Divulge vb.	reveal, disclose, expose
Do vb.	execute, enact, carry out, finish, attain
Do away with vb. phr.	kill, murder
Do over vb. phr.	redo, rework, repeat, redecorate, remodel

Doctrine n.	teaching, teachings, belief, principle, dogma
Docile adj.	yielding, tame
Dogmatic adj.	authoritarian, domineering, overbearing
Dole n.	alms, relief, welfare **vb.** distribute, mete out
Doleful adj.	sorrowful, mournful, dejected
Domesticate vb.	tame, train, teach
Dominate vb.	control, rule, govern, subjugate
Donation n.	gift, contribution, present, offering
Doom n.	fate, destiny, fortune
Doomed adj.	destined, fated, foreordained
Doubt vb.	distrust, mistrust **n.** skepticism
Doubtful adj.	uncertain, questionable, undetermined
Doubtless adv.	unquestionable, certainly, positively, assuredly
Douse vb.	immerse, submerge, put under water
Dowdy adj.	untidy, messy, sloppy, unkempt
Downcast adj.	dejected, depressed, downhearted, crestfallen
Downfall n.	comedown, destruction
Downgrade vb.	lower, reduce, decrease, diminish
Downhearted adj.	sad, gloomy, depressed, downcast
Downpour n.	deluge, flood
Downright adv.	completely, totally, absolutely, positively

Drain vb.	empty, tap, sap n. tap, duct, channel
Drama n.	play, piece, show, production
Dramatist n.	playwright
Draw vb.	sketch, trace, depict, picture, drag
Drawback vb. phr.	withdraw, recoil, retreat
Dread vb.	fear n. fear, terror
Dreadful adj.	terrible, awful, frightful, horrible, awe-inspiring
Dream n.	reverie, daydream, fancy vb. imagine, fantasize, invent, fancy
Dreary adj.	dismal, gloomy, cheerless, depressing
Drench vb.	soak, wet, bathe
Dress n.	frock, costume vb. clothe, garb
Drift vb.	float, sail, wander
Drifter n.	vagabond, tramp
Drink vb.	sip, gulp, imbibe n. swallow, sip, gulp
Drive vb.	control, direct, impel, push, propel n. ride, journey, trip, outing, tour
Droop vb.	sag, sink
Drop vb.	fall, tumble n. drip, trickle
Drowsy adj.	sleepy, lethargic, lulling, comatose
Drudgery n.	toil, labour, travail
Drug n.	medicine, remedy vb. anesthetize
Drugged adj.	doped, stupefied, groggy
Drunk adj.	intoxicated, inebriated, soused

Dry adj.	arid, dehydrated, parched, desiccate
Dubious adj.	doubtful, uncertain, wavering
Dumb adj.	dull, stupid, ignorant
Dunce adj.	half-wit, stupid
Dungeon n.	prison, cell, jail
Dupe vb.	cheat, deceive, beguile, gull
Duplicate vb.	copy, relicate, reproduce **n.** copy, clone, replica, facsimile
Durable adj.	lasting, firm
Duress n.	constraint, restraint, captivity
Dutiful adj.	faithful
Duty n.	obligation, faithfulness, conscience
Dwarf n.	midget
Dwelling n.	residence, home, abode, house
Dwindle vb.	diminish, wane, lessen, decrease

E

Eager adj.	keen, fervent, enthusiastic
Earnest adj.	sincere, serious, determined
Earthly adj.	worldly, everyday, mundane, material
Earthy adj.	earthlike, crude, unrefined, vulgar
Ease n.	comfort, rest, relaxation, contentment **vb.** comfort, relieve, soothe, lighten
Easy adj.	simple, effortless, comfortable, leisurely
Eat vb.	consume, chew, devour, swallow

Ebb vb.	recede, drawback **n.** low tide, neap
Ebullient adj.	buoyant, high-spirited, vivacious, exuberant
Economical adj.	thrifty, provident, sparing, careful, frugal
Economize vb.	save
Edifice n.	building, structure
Edit vb.	revise and correct, amend, condense
Educate vb.	teach, train, instruct, school
Education n.	instruction, training, schooling, culture, learning
Eerie adj.	weird, strange
Effect n.	result, outcome **vb.** accomplish, achieve, cause, make
Effective adj.	productive, efficient, practical
Efficient adj.	effective, useful, competent, apt, adept, able, capable, talented, skilled, clever
Effigy n.	image, figure, statue
Effloresce vb.	bloom, flower
Effort n.	endeavour, attempt
Effortless adj.	easy, simple
Effusive adj.	lavish, generous, exuberant, widely, diffused
Egoism n.	selfishness, self-interest, egotism, conceit, pride
Egotism n.	self-importance, self-conceit, self-praise, egoism, conceit
Elaborate adj.	ornate, ornamented, decorated

Elastic adj.	flexible, resilient
Elated adj.	overjoyed, happy, ecstatic, jubilant
Elderly adj.	old, aged, aging, superannuated **n.** grace, refinement, polish, beauty
Elegiac adj.	mournful, sorrowful, plaintive
Elegant adj.	fine, refined, tasteful
Elementary adj.	basic, primary, fundamental, simple
Elevate vb.	raise, lift
Elicit vb.	evoke, bring out, tract, bring to light
Eligible adj.	fit to be chosen, legally qualified
Eliminate vb.	remove, get rid of, leave out, omit
Elite n.	upperclass, aristocracy, nobility, gentry
Elixir adj.	compound, refined, quintessence
Elliptic(al) adj.	like an ellipse, incomplete, containing, omission
Eloquent adj.	articulate
Elucidate vb.	explain, illustrate, unfold, make clear, clarify, demonstrate
Elude vb.	evade, avoid
Emaciated adj.	shrivelled, shrunken, haggard, lean, thin
Emancipation n.	liberation, release, deliverance
Embalm vb.	preserve, cherish, enshrine, preserve, from decay
Embargo n.	restriction, restraint, prohibition
Embarrass vb.	shame, abash

Embassy n.	consulate
Embellish vb.	decorate, adorn, ornament
Embezzle vb.	misappropriate, misuse, rob, pilfer
Emblem n.	sign, token, symbol, badge, mark
Embrace vb.	hug, clasp
Emerge vb.	come forth, appear
Eminent adj.	distinguished, celebrated, renowned, important, prominent
Emit vb.	discharge, expel, eject, emanate
Emphasis n.	stress, accent
Emphatic adj.	forceful, strong
Employ vb.	use, utilise, engage, retain
Employee n.	worker, labourer, wage-earner
Employer n.	proprietor, management, manager
Employment n.	work, job, position
Empty adj.	vacant, unoccupied, void, blank **vb.** void, unload, evacuate
Emulate vb.	vie with, compete with, survive to equal or to excel
Enchant vb.	charm, fascinate, bewitch
Enclose vb.	surround, encircle
Encore adv. fr.	Again, once more, call back, recall
Encounter vb.	meet, come across
Encourage vb.	support, inspire
Encumbrance n.	impediment, hindrance, hampering
Endanger vb.	imperil, jeopardise, risk
Endeavour vb.	try, attempt, struggle **n.** try, attempt
Endorse vb.	superscribe, ratify, confirm

Endow vb.	give, bestow
Endure vb.	last, continue, persists
Enemy n.	foe, adversary, opponent, antagonist
Energetic adj.	vigorous, active
Energy n.	power, force, strength, vigour
Enervate vb.	enfeeble, debilitate, devitalize
Engage vb.	employ, hire, retain
Engaged adj.	betrothed, occupied, busy
Engaging adj.	beguiling, charming
Engross vb.	absorb, occupy, take up
Enigma n.	mystery, riddle, conundrum
Enigmatic adj.	puzzling, perplex, baffling, confusing
Enkindle vb.	inflame, ignite, kindle, incite, excite, rouse, instigate, provoke, stir up
Enjoyment n.	delight, pleasure, gratification
Enlarge vb.	increase, amplify, expand, magnify
Enlighten vb.	inform, tech, educate
Enlist vb.	enroll, enter, sign up, register
Enormity n.	wickedness, heinousness, barbarity
Enormous adj.	huge, immense, vast, colossal
Enrage vb.	infuriate, anger, madden
Enroll vb.	enlist, register, sign up
Ensue vb.	arise, result
Enterprise n.	project, venture, undertaking
Enterprising adj.	resourceful, energetic
Entertain vb.	amuse, divert, interest
Enthusiasm n.	eagerness, zeal, earnestness

Enthusiastic adj.	eager, zealous, earnest
Entice vb.	allure, lure, attract, tempt
Entire adj.	complete, undivided
Entitle vb.	authorize, allow, empower
Entourage n.	retinue, company, escort, cortege
Entrance n.	entry, door, access, gate, opening
Entreat vb.	beg, plead, implore
Entreaty n.	appeal, plea
Entrust vb.	delegate, commit, consign, assign
Entwine vb.	twist, together, twine, encircle
Enumerate vb.	count, number, list
Environment n.	surroundings, habitat, conditions, atmosphere
Environs n. pl.	neighbourhood, vicinity
Envision vb.	imagine, dream up, envisage, visualise
Envoy n.	jealousy, covetousness
Ephemeral adj.	short-lived, transitory, transient, fleeting
Epidemic n.	scourge, pestilence
Episode n.	event, incident
Equal adj.	equivalent, identical
Error n.	mistake, oversight, inaccuracy
Erudite adj.	learned, sage, wise, well-educated, scholarly
Eschew vb.	avoid, shun
Escort n.	convoy, guide vb. accompany, attend, usher

Essence n.	principle, basis
Essential adj.	important, necessary, vital, indispensable
Establish vb.	found, set up
Esteem vb.	value, regard, highly, revere, respect **n.** reverence, regard, honour
Estimate vb.	value, gauge, judge, evaluate **n.** value, evaluation, computation
Estimation n.	judgment, point of view
Ethereal adj.	celestial, heavenly
Etiquette n.	decorum, manners
Eulogy n.	speech, discourse, praise, laudation, applause, commendation
Euphemism n.	expression, substitution of an inoffensive or unpleasant word
Evade vb.	elude, avoid, escape
Evaluate vb.	appraise, value
Event n.	occurrence, incident, episode
Eventual adj.	ultimate, consequent
Ever adv.	always, continuously, constantly, at all, at anytime
Everlasting adj.	eternal, endless, perpetual
Everyday adj.	common, commonplace, ordinary, usual, customary
Evidence n.	proof, testimony, grounds, indication, sign
Evident adj.	clear, plain, obvious, apparent

Evil adj.	sinful, immoral, wicked, bad, harmful, injurious **n.** harm, woe, badness, wickedness, sin
Evolve adj.	develop, grow, emerge, result, unroll, unfold
Exact adj.	correct, accurate, errorless, faultless
Exaggerate vb.	overstate, magnify
Exalt vb.	raise, elevate, erect, lift up, heighten, make lofty, praise, magnify, glorify, dignify, aggrandize, elevate
Examine vb.	inspect, investigate, scrutinize
Excavate vb.	dig, burrow, hollow, hollow out, expose by digging, scoop out
Exceed vb.	beat, surpass, outdo, excel
Excel vb.	outdo, surpass, exceed, transcend, cap, go beyond, take precedence
Excellence n.	superiority, distinction
Excellent adj.	fine, superior, wonderful, marvelous
Except prep.	but, same, barring, excluding
Exceptional adj.	unusual, different, irregular, strange, abnormal
Excerpt n.	extract, piece, abstract
Excess adj.	profuse, abundant, immoderate **n.** profusion, lavishness
Exchange vb.	trade, swap, barter **n.** trade, interchange, market
Excite vb.	stir up, arouse, stimulate, move, animate, incide
Exclamation n.	outcry, shout, clamour

Exclude vb.	deep out, shut out, clamour
Exclude vb.	deep out, shut out, bar, except
Exclusive adj.	limited, restricted, restrictive, selective, select, fashionable, choice
Excruciating adj.	torturing, tormenting, agonizing, very painful
Excursion n.	trip, tour, voyage, outing
Excuse vb.	forgive, pardon n. explanation, reason, pleas, apology
Execute vb.	carry out, do, complete, achieve, accomplish, kill, put to death, hang
Exemplary adj.	worthy of imitation, fit for a pattern, remarkably good, highly virtuous, correct, commendable
Exempt vb.	relieve, release, free, let off, liberated, grant immunity to, exonerate
Exercise n.	practice, drill, training, gymnastics, calisthenics, use, application, employment, train, drill, practice
Exertion n.	effort, attempt, endeavour, strain
Exhaust vb.	tie, fatigue, wear out, use, use up, consume, spend
Exhaustive adj.	thorough, comprehensive, complete, thorough-going, extensive
Exhibit vb.	show, display, demonstrate, show, display, betray, reveal n. show, display, demonstration, exhibition
Exonerate vb.	clear, acquit
Exorbitant adj.	outrageous, excessive, unreasonable, preposterous

Exotic adj.	strange, foreign, alien, unknown
Expand vb.	enlarge, swell, inflate, bloat
Expect vb.	anticipate, await, look forward to
Expedite vb.	hasten, rush, hurry, speedup
Expedition n.	journey, voyage, trip, excursion
Expel vb.	banish, deport, exile, driver out or away, discharge
Expend vb.	use, consume, exhaust
Expense n.	cost, price, charge, payment
Expensive adj.	costly, high-priced, dear
Experience n.	encountering, living, existence, knowledge, background, skill **vb.** feel, live, through, undergo
Expert n.	authority, specialist **adj.** skilful, experienced, knowledgeable, skilled
Explain vb.	clarify, define, interpret, justify, account for
Explanation n.	description, definition, interpretation, account, justification, reason, excuse
Explicit adj.	clear, plain, expressive, definite, unambiguous, unreserved, straightforward
Exploit n.	feat, accomplishment, achievement
Explore vb.	investigate, examine
Expose vb.	reveal, bare, uncover, disclose, display
Express vb.	state, declare **adj.** specific, precise, exact, special, non-stop, quick, rapid, fast, direct

Expression n.	statement, declaration, look, air
Expunge vb.	erase, obliterate, delete, blot out, rub out, strike out, efface, cancel, destroy, wipe out
Exquisite adj.	delicate, dainty, elegant, beautiful, fine, excellent, superb, matchless, perfect
Extempore adv.	suddenly, offhand, without preparation, on the spur of the moment
Extend vb.	stretch, stretch out, lengthen, give, offer, grant, yield
Extension n.	stretching, expansion, enlargement, increase
Extensive adj.	wide, broad, spacious, vast
Extent n.	degree, measure, amount, range
Extenuate vb.	lessen, diminish, reduce in size or bulk, mitigate, excuse, apologise for, palliate
Exterior n.	outside, face, surface, covering **adj.** outside, outer, external
Exterminate vb.	kill, slay, put to death, eradicate, eliminate
External adj.	exterior, outer, outside
Extinct adj.	dead, lost, gone, vanished
Extinguish vb.	quench, put out, quell, douse, suppress, stifle, smother, suffocate
Extract vb.	draw out, withdraw, pull out, remove **n.** essence, distillate
Extradite vb.	deliver, surrender, deport

Extraordinary adj.	unusual, exceptional, rare, uncommon, remarkable
Extravagant adj.	wasteful, lavish, excessive
Extreme adj.	utmost, greatest, furthest, outermost, endmost, ultimate, excessive, immoderate **n.** end, limit, extremity
Exuberant adj.	ebullient, high-spirited, buoyant, vivacious
Exult vb.	rejoice, delight
Exultation n.	joy, delight, triumph, elation

F

Fabric n.	cloth, material, textile
Fabricate vb.	make, manufacture, assemble, form, construct
Fabulous adj.	fantastic, unbelievable, amazing, astonishing, astounding
Face n.	look, expression, features, visage, countenance, front, façade **vb.** meet, encounter, comfort
Facilitate vb.	make easy, render, less difficult
Facility n.	easy, skill, skillfulness, ability, equipment, material
Facsimile n.	exact copy, duplicate, reproduction
Fact n.	truth, certainty, actuality, reality

Factual adj.	correct, accurate, true
Faculty n.	ability, capacity, talent
Fade vb.	pale, bleach, discolour, diminish, weaken, fail
Fail vb.	fall short, miss, founder, disappoint, fade, weaken, dwindle
Failure n.	failing, unsuccessfulness, deficiency, insufficiency
Faint adj.	dim, faded, indistinct, feeble, weak, halfhearted **vb.** swoon, lose consciousness, collapse
Fair n.	exhibit, exhibition, festival, bazaar, carnival
Faith n.	trust, reliance, belief, belief, religion, creed
Faithful adj.	loyal, devoted, trustworthy, trusty, true, credible, accurate, strict
Faithless adj.	disloyal, treacherous, perfidious, unfaithful, untrue
Fake adj.	false, pretended, phony **n.** fraud, cheat, counterfeit, forgery, imitation
Fall vb.	drop, descend, plunge, topple, die, decrease, diminish **n.** autumn, drip, decline, spill, collapse
Fallible n.	imperfect, weak, liable to error or mistake
Falter vb.	stumble, hesitate, tremble
Fame n.	name, reputation, renown, honour, glory

Famed adj.	renowned, known, famous
Familiarity n.	knowledge, understanding, awareness, comprehension
Family n.	relatives, tribe, relations, house
Famine vb.	want, hunger, starvation
Famish adj.	starve, kill or destroy by hunger
Famous adj.	well-known, renowned, celebrated, famed, eminent, illustrious
Fan vb.	follower, enthusiast, devotee, afficionado
Fancy n.	imagination, fantasy, taste **adj.** ornate, ornamented, elaborate, special deluxe
Fantastic adj.	unbelievable, incredible, unreal, unimaginable
Fantasy n.	illusion, mirage, daydream, delusion, vision, dream
Fascinate vb.	attract, charm, bewitch, enchant
Fashionable adj.	stylish, chic, modish, smart
Fasten vb.	attach, fix, join, secure, pin
Fastidious adj.	difficult, squeamish, queasy, delicate, exquisite, precious, hard to please, over-delicate
Fat adj.	fatty, oily, greasy, obese, plump, fleshy, stout, chubby, thick, wide
Fatal adj.	deadly, lethal, mortal, fatal, doomed, inevitable
Fate n.	fortune, luck, chance, destiny
Fatigue n.	weariness, exhaustion, tiredness

Fault n.	defect, imperfection, flaw, blemish, weakness, blame, responsibility
Faulty adj.	defective, imperfect, damaged, broken
Fear adj.	fright, dread, terror, alarm, dismay, anxiety **vb.** dread, be afraid of
Fearless adj.	brave, courageous, bold
Feast n.	banquet, dinner, party, barbecue **vb.** dine, gluttonize
Feat n.	achievement, act, deed
Feature n.	quality, characteristic, trait **vb.** star, promote
Fee n.	pay, payment, remuneration
Feeble adj.	weak, frail, sickly, infirm
Feed vb.	nourish, satisfy **n.** fodder, forage, food
Feel vb.	experience, sense, perceive
Feign vb.	pretend, invent, fabricate, affect, make a show of
Felicitation n.	welcome, congratulation
Fertile adj.	productive, rich, fruitful
Fervour n.	heat, warmth, ardor, intensity, eagerness
Festive adj.	merry, gay, joyful, joyous
Fetching adj.	attractive, charming, pleasing
Feud n.	quarrel, argument, dispute, strife
Fiasco n.	failure, abortive, attempt
Fictitious adj.	madeup, invented, fabricated, imaginary, make-believe

Fight n.	battle, war, conflict, combat **vb.** combat, battle, struggle
Filter n.	strainer, sieve, screen
Filth adj.	dirt, foulness, pollution, sewage
Filthy adj.	dirty, foul, polluted, contaminated
Final adj.	last, ultimate, terminal, concluding
Finally adv.	at last, in the end, at long last, ultimately, eventually
Fine adj.	excellent, superior, superb, choice, exquisite, perfect, thin, minute, powdered
Firm adj.	rigid, stiff, unchanging, inflexible, stead-fast, unshakeable, compact, dense, hard **n.** company, business, concern, partnership, corporation
Firmament n.	sky, the heavens
Fissure n.	cleft, crevice, chink, crack, break, breach, gap, opening, chasm, rift, fracture
Fitting vb.	attach, rivet, cement, fasten, pin, tie, secure, affix, repair, mend, determine, establish, pinpoint
Flair n.	flamboyance, style, drama, panache, elan, dash
Flamboyant adj.	flashy, gaudy, showy, ostentatious
Flame n.	fire, blaze
Flat adj.	level, even, smooth, dull, uninteresting, boring, lifeless **adv.** evenly, smoothly

Flaw n.	imperfection, sport, fault, blemish, defect
Flecked adj.	spotted, streaked, striped, mottled, variegated
Flee vb.	run away, desert, escape
Fleet adj.	swift, fast, rapid, quick
Fleeting adj.	temporary, brief, passing, swift
Flexible adj.	elastic, supple, pliant, pliable, yielding, easy, agreeable, adaptable
Flimsy adj.	weak, frail fragile, wobby
Flourish vb.	grow, succeed, prosper, wave, brandish
Flout vb.	scorn, disdain, ignore, fly in the face of, spurn
Flow vb.	stream, pour, run, spurt, squirt, gush, spout **n.** deluge, overflow, inundated
Fluent adj.	flowing, glib
Fluid n.	liquid, gas **adj.** liquid, liquefied, running, gaseous
Flurry n.	calm **vb.** compose
Flush adj.	even, level, flat
Fluster vb.	agitate, confuse, flurry, make nervous or uneasy, rattle, upset
Foe n.	enemy, adversary, antagonist, opponent
Foliage n.	leaves, cluster of leaves, leafage
Follow n.	succeed, ensue, obey, heed, observe, chase, purse, track, trace
Follower n.	pupil, disciple

Following n.	supporters, disciples, public
Folly n.	silliness, blunder, stupidity, absurdity, foolishness
Fond adj.	attached, affectionate, loving, tender, affectionate
Food n.	sustenance, bread, victuals, provisions
Foolish adj.	silly, senseless, stupid, simple
Footing n.	basis, foundation, base
Forbid vb.	ban, disallow, prohibit, prevent
Forbidding adj.	unfriendly, hostile, sinister, evil
Forceful adj.	vigorous, energetic, dynamic
Foreboding n.	suspicion, apprehension, misgiving
Forecast n.	Foresight, prophecy, prevision, provident
Forego vb.	relinquish, resign, renounce, surrender, cede, yield, abandon, give up, let go, part with
Foreman n.	supervisor, superindendent, overseer
Foremost n.	first, leading, most advanced, front
Forest n.	wood, woods, wood-land, grove, copse
Forestall vb.	prevent, hinder, obstruct, thwart
Foretell vb.	predict, prophesy, divine
Forgive vb.	pardon, excuse
Forgo vb.	release, relinquish
Forlorn adj.	deserted, abandoned, forsaken, solitary, lost
Formal adj.	conventional, conformist, ceremonial, ritual

Former adj.	previous, earlier, erstwhile, one-time
Formidable adj.	imposing, alarming, terrifying, frightful, terrible, horrifying
Forsake vb.	desert, give up, abandon, forgo
Forth adv.	forward, onward, out
Forthright adj.	direct, honest, candid, frank, outspoken
Fortify vb.	strengthen, bolster, butteress
Fortunate adj.	lucky, blessed, charmed, auspicious, favorable
Fortune n.	luck, chance, lot, fate, wealth, riches
Forward adv.	onward, ahead **adj.** front, first, leading, foremost, rude, bold, arrogant, fresh, impertinent, impudent
Foul adj.	dirty, filthy, unclean, impure, polluted, evil, wicked, vile, sinful, stormy, bad, rainy
Found vb.	establish, organize
Foundation vb.	basis, establishment, ground
Fountainhead n.	source, origin, cause, fountain, first, principle
Foxy adj.	crafty, sly, cunning, artful, wily, shrews, sharp, canny
Fracture n.	break, crack, rupture **vb.** break, crack, rupture
Fragile adj.	delicate, breakable, frail, weak
Fragment n.	bit, part, piece, scrap, remnant
Fragrance n.	smell, odour, aroma, perfume, scent
Fragrant adj.	sweet-smelling, perfumed, aromatic, scented

Frail adj.	weak, fragile, breakable, feeble, delicate
Frank adj.	candid, open, forthright, honest, unreserved, direct, sincere
Frantic adj.	wild, frenzied, delirious, excited, hysterical, mad, crazy
Fraud n.	deceit, trickery, treachery
Fraudulent adj.	fake, deceitful, tricky, dishonest
Freak n.	monster, abnormality, oddity, curiosity
Freedom n.	liberty, independence
Freely adv.	generously, liberally, unstintingly
Freight n.	cargo, load, shipping, shipment
Frenzy n.	excitement, agitation, craze
Frequent adj.	common, customary, habitual **vb.** habituate, visit, often
Fret vb.	worry, anguish, grieve, torment
Fright n.	fear, terror, alarm, panic
Frighten vb.	alarm, scare, terrify, panic
Frigid adj.	icy, freezing, cold, frosty, wintry, glacial, arctic
Fringe n.	border, edge, hem, edge, hem, edging, trimming
Frisky adj.	lively, vivacious, active, spirited, animated, peppy, gay
Frolic vb.	frisk, cavort, play, gambol, romp
Front n.	face, façade, beginning, start, head **vb.** face, border, look out on

Frontier n.	boundary, border
Frugality n.	thriftiness, thrift, economy
Fruitful adj.	fertile, productive, rich, abundant
Fruitless adj.	defeat, discourage, prevent, disappoint, baffle, disconcert
Full adj.	filled, complete, replete, take, occupied, in use
Full-grown adj.	mature, ripe, adult, complete
Fume n.	smoke, vapor, steam, gas **vb.** smoke, rage, rave, storm
Fun n.	pleasure, entertainment, amusement, merriment, sport, enjoyment, gaiety
Function n.	use, activity, operation, ceremony, affair, celebration, party, gathering **vb.** operate, work, run
Fundamental adj.	basic, elementary, essential, principal, underlying, primary **vb.** basics, elements, essential, principal
Funny adj.	humourous, amusing, droll, comic, comical, laughable
Furious adj.	enraged, angry
Furnish vb.	supply, provide, decorate, appoint, outfit
Furore n.	tumult, commotion, turmoil, to-do
Fusion n.	liquefaction, melting, amalgamation, blending, union, intermingling, intermixture, coalition, merging
Fuss n.	bother, ado, commotion **vb.** bother, annoy, pester, irritate

Fusty adj.	musty, mouldy, ill-smelling, malodorous
Futile adj.	useless, pointless, vain, idle, worthless, unimportant, minor, trivial

G

Gaiety n.	cheerfulness, high spirits, high-spiritedness, joyfulness
Gala n.	festival, fete, carnival, ball, party
Galaxy n.	cosmic system, milky, way
Gall vb.	irritate, vex, annoy, provoke, anger
Gallant adj.	brave, valiant, valorous, bold, courageous, polite, courteous, noble
Galvanize vb.	electrify, excite, bring to a mock vitality, change with electricity
Gamble vb.	bet, wager, game, risk, hazard, venture n. chance, risk
Gambol n.	frisk, cavort, play, frolic, romp
Game n.	amusement, play, sport, pastime, entertainment, contest, competition
Gang n.	band, troop, group, company, crew, horde
Gangster n.	crook, criminal, gunman
Gap n.	space, interval, break
Garbage n.	trash, rubbish, refuse, waste
Garbled adj.	distorted, twisted, mixed-up, confused
Garrulous adj.	talkative, loquacious

Gasp vb.	puff, pant, wheeze
Gather vb.	assemble, collect, accumulate, come or bring together, assume, understand, learn
Gaudy adj.	flashy, showy, ostentatious, bold, loud
Gaze vb.	stare, gape, goggle at, look
General adj.	indefinite, miscellaneous, inexact, vague, common, usual, regular, customary
Generate vb.	create, produce, make
Generous vb.	charitable, liberal, unselfish, noble, big, honourable
Genius n.	ability, talent, intellect, gift, aptitude, prodigy, brain
Gentle adj.	friendly, amiable, mild, kindly, kind, tame, cultivated, civilised
Genuine adj.	real, actual, true, sincere, unaffected, definite
Gesture n.	movement, move, sign, signal **vb.** motion, signal
Get by vb. phr.	manage, survive
Get in vb. phr.	enter, arrive
Get off vb. phr.	disembark, alight
Get over vb. phr.	overcome, recover, survive
Get up vb. phr.	arise, rise
Ghastly adj.	horrifying, horrible, macabre, frightful, frightening, hideous, dreadful, grisly, pale, wan, white, deathly

Ghost n.	specter, phantom, spirit, spook, trace, vestige, hint, suggestion
Giant n.	colossus, goliath, monster **adj.** gigantic, huge, colossal, enormous, monstrous
Gift n.	present, offering, donation, talent, genius, ability, aptitude
Gifted adj.	talent, able, ingenious
Gigantic adj.	huge, enormous, giant, large
Gingerly adj.	cautiously, daintly, gentle **adv.** carefully, cautiously, gently
Give away vb. phr.	betray, reveal, divulge
Give in vb. phr.	yield, submit, surrender, admit
Give off vb. phr.	emit, give off
Glad adj.	pleased, happy, satisfied, delighted, happy, joyous, joyful, cheerful
Glamour n.	allure, charm, attraction
Glance vb.	peek, glimpse, look, reflect, rebound, ricochet **n.** peek, glimpse, look
Glare n.	dazzle, flash, brilliance, **vb.** scowl, start
Glaring adj.	obvious, prominent, flagrant, blatant
Glassy adj.	vacant, empty, blank, emotionless
Glide vb.	slide, slip, flow
Glimpse n.	peck, glance, impression
Glitter vb.	sparkle, glisten, shimmer, glimmer, shine **n.** light, splendor
Global adj.	worldwise, universal, international

Globule n.	small, round particle, drop, bead, little, globe
Gloom n.	darkness, shade, shadowy, dimness, sadness, melancholy
Glory n.	honour, eminence, renown, splendor, magnificence, grandeur
Glossary n.	lexicon, dictionary
Glossy adj.	shiny, smooth, polished, glistening, sleek
Glower vb.	share, glare, scowl, look back, look fierce
Glow n.	gleam, light, warmth, hear **vb.** gleam, glimmer, shine, radiate, shine
Gluttony n.	swinishness, insatiability, hoggishness, piggishness
Gnaw vb.	eat, chew, erode
Goad vb.	prod, stimulate, spur, incite, provoke
Good-humoured adj.	cheerful, pleasant, sunny, amiable, good-natured
Gorgeous adj.	splendid, magnificent, grand, dazzling
Gossip n.	hearsay, rumour, prattle, prate, snoop, tattler **vb.** prattle, tattle, chatter, blab
Govern vb.	rule, control, guide, run, command
Gown n.	dress, frock, robe
Grab vb.	seize, clutch, grasp
Grace n.	gracefulness, ease, elegance, charm, attractiveness, beauty
Gracious adj.	kind, friendly, courteous, polite, tender, merciful, mild, gentle

Gradual adj.	slow, little by little, moderate
Graft n.	cheating, fraud, dishonesty, theft, corruption
Grand adj.	splendid, elaborate, great, royal, stately, fine, noble, dignified, chief, principal, main
Grandiloquent adj.	bombastic, pompous, inflated, stilted, tumid, high-flown
Grant vb.	give, bestow, confer, award, agree, allow, concede
Grasping adj.	greedy, acquisitive, selfish, possessive
Grateful adj.	appreciate, thankful
Gratify vb.	satisfy, please
Gratifying adj.	pleasing, agreeable, delightful, satisfactory
Grave adj.	sober, thoughtful, solemn, serious, important, serious, weighty
Gravity n.	seriousness, importance, concern
Greed n.	avarice, greediness, covetousness
Greedy n.	avarice, greediness, covetous, grasping, avaricious
Green adj.	inexperienced, naïve, unsophisticated, amateurish
Grief n.	sorrow, sadness, distress, suffering, anguish, woe, misery
Grieve vb.	lament, mourn, weep, distress, sorrow, sadden, hurt

Grievous adj.	dreadful, awful, gross, shameful, outrageous, regrettable, lamentable
Grim adj.	stern, severe, harsh, sad, ghastly, sinister, frightful, horrible
Grimace n.	distortion of countenance, smirk, wry face
Grimy adj.	foul, begrimed, defiled, dirty, filthy, full of grime
Grind vb.	powder, pulverize, mill, crush, sharpen, smooth, even
Groan vb.	moan, sob
Groove n.	slot, channel, scratch, furrow
Grotesque adj.	weird, bizarre, strange, odd, peculiar, freakish, queer
Grouchy adj.	grumpy, cantankerous, surly
Groundwork n.	base, basis, background, foundation, support, bottom, ground, source, origin, basis, first principal
Growth n.	increase, development
Grudge n.	Resentment, ill will, spite, bitterness
Gruesome adj.	ghastly, hideous, horrifying, horrible
Grumble vb.	complain, protest, fuss
Grumpy adj.	grouchy, cantankerous, surly
Guard vb.	protect, preserve, shield, defend **n.** watchman, sentry, protector, sentinel
Guarded adj.	careful, cautious, discreet
Guess vb.	suppose, think, imagine, believe **n.** notion, opinion, hypothesis, theory

Guide vb.	lead, direct, conduct, steer, pilot, influence, affect **n.** director, pilot, simple
Guilt n.	blame, fault, sin, offense, misstep
Guilty adj.	responsible, culpable, blameworthy
Gulf n.	chasm, abyss, ravine, canyon, inlet, sound, bay
Gusto n.	relish, zest, pleasure, enjoyment
Gutter n.	drain, trough, ditch, sewer

H

Habit n.	addiction, compulsion, disposition, custom, practice
Habitat n.	natural locality (of a plant or an animal), area of distribution
Habitation n.	dwelling, abode, home
Habituate vb.	accustom, familiarise, use, train, harden
Hale adj.	hearty, healthy, robust, vigorous
Hall n.	passage, corridor, hallway, vestibule, lobby, foyer
Hallucination n.	mirage, illusion, vision, dream, fantasy
Halt vb.	stop, cease, hold **n.** stop, end
Hamper vb.	hinder, prevent, obstruct, thwart **n.** basket, creel
Hand down vb. phr.	pass on, bequeath, give

Hand out vb. phr.	distribute, pass out
Handicap n.	disadvantage, hindrance
Handsome adj.	good-looking, fine, comely, generous, large, big, liberal, ample
Handy adj.	ready, at hand, near, near by, close, helpful, clever, useful
Hang vb.	suspend, dangle, drape, execute, kill, lynch
Happen vb.	occur, take place, come to pass
Happiness n.	joy, delight, joyfulness, elation, joyousness, ecstasy
Happy adj.	pleased, contended, satisfied, lucky, fortune
Harbinger n.	forerunner, precursor, herald
Habour n.	port, haven, anchorage **vb.** shelter, protect
Hard up adj. phr.	up against it, poor, poverty-stricken, broke
Hard-boiled adj.	tough, unsympathetic, harsh, unsentimental
Harden vb.	solidify, petrify
Hardheaded adj.	obstinate, stubborn, headstrong, unyielding
Hard hearted adj.	hard, stony-hearted, merciless, unmerciful, ruthless, pitiless, callous
Hardly adv.	scarcely, barely
Hard-nosed adj.	tough, practical, shrewd, businesslike
Hardship n.	difficulty, trouble, affliction

Harmful adj.	mischievous, hurtful, injurious
Harmless adj.	innocent, painless
Harmonise vb.	adapt, attune, reconcile, accord, agree, be in unison
Harmonious adj.	melodious, tuneful, amicable, congenial
Harmony n.	agreement, accord, unity
Harness vb.	yoke, control,
Haste n.	rush, hurry, flurry, rush, heedlessness
Hasten vb.	hurry, rush, run, scurry, dash, scamper, sprint, hurry, rush, dispatch, quicken, urge, press, speed
Hat n.	bonnet, headgear, headpiece, helmet
Hate vb.	detest, abhor, loathe, despise, disfavour, dislike **n.** hatred, loathing, abhorrence, dislike
Hateful adj.	detestable, loathsome, offensive
Hatred n.	hate, loathing, aversion
Haughty adj.	aloof, proud, prideful, arrogant
Haul vb.	drag, draw, pull, tow
Haven n.	harbour, port, shelter, asylum, place of safety
Havoc n.	ruin, devastation, destruction, carnage
Hawk vb.	cry, sell by out-cry, peddle
Hawk-eyed adj.	sharp, sighted, keen-eyed, eagle eyed, discerning, penetrating, astute, sagacious, keen

Hazard n.	peril, risk, danger **vb.** offer, tender, dare
Hazardous adj.	perilous, dangerous, risky
Headway n.	progress, movement, advance
Heady adj.	intoxicating, thrilling, electrifying, exciting
Heal vb.	cure, restore
Healthy adj.	hale, hearty, robust, vigorous, strong, sound, healthful
Heap n.	pile, stack, mound, collection, accumulation **vb.** pile, stack, mound, collect, accumulate
Hear vb.	listen, hearken, detect, perceive
Heart n.	center, core, sympathy, feeling, sentiment
Heartless adj.	cruel, mean, hard, hearted, ruthless, pitiless
Heated adj.	fiery, vehement, intense, passionate
Heave vb.	hoist, boost, raise, haul, pull, tug
Heaven n.	paradise, empyrean
Heavenly adj.	blissful, divine, saintly, angelic, holy, blessed, celestial
Heavy adj.	weighty, ponderous, intense, concentrated, severe, burdensome, oppressive, harsh, depressing, sad, serious, oppressed, grave, gloomy, mournful, melancholy, dismal, boring, dull, tiresome
Hackle vb.	harry, hector, torment, tease, harass

Heed vb.	obey, regard, observe **n.** attention, mind
Heedful adj.	observant, mindful, regardful, cautious, attentive, wary, circumspect, watchful
Heedless adj.	unmindful, disregardful, deaf, blind, inattentive
Height n.	attitude, elevation, tallness, mountain, peak, prominence, acme, pinnacle, maximum
Heighten vb.	intensify, increase, amplify, concentrate, focus
Heinous adj.	grievous, abominable, atrocious
Hello interj.	hi!, hiya!, greetings, good morning, good afternoon, good evening
Help vb.	aid, assist, support, back, encourage, avoid, prevent, wait on, attend, serve **n.** aid, assistance, support, relief
Helper n.	assistant, aide, supporter
Helpful adj.	advantageous, profitable, valuable
Helpless adj.	dependant, feeble, weak, disabled, unresourceful, incompetent, inept, incapable
Herd n.	flock, crowd, group, drove, pack **vb.** group, gather, crowd
Heritage n.	legacy, birthright, inheritance, patrimony
Hermit n.	anchorite, recluse, eremite
Hero adj.	champion, idol, paladin

Heroic adj.	valiant, brave, valorous, dauntless, gallant, courageous, bold, fearless
Heroism n.	bravery, valour, gallantry, courage, boldness
Hesitate vb.	pause, delay, wait, doubt, waver, be doubtful, stop to consider
Heterogeneous adj.	unlike, dissimilar, different, diverse, miscellaneous, mixed, contrary, contrast, opposed
Hibernate vb.	pass the winter, lie torpid in winter
Hide vb.	conceal, cover, mask, screen, camouflage, cloak, shroud, veil **n.** skin, pelt, leather, fur
Hideous adj.	ugly, frightful, frightening, shocking, horrible, horrifying, terrible, terrifying, gross, monstrous, grisly
Highly adv.	very, exceedingly, extremely, extraordinary
High-handed adj.	overbearing, oppressive, violent, despotic, self-willed, domineering
High-minded adj.	noble, lofty, honourable
High-priced adj.	expensive, dear, costly
High-strung adj.	tense, nervous, intense, wrought-up
Highway n.	speedway, parkway, freeway, skyway, superhighway, turnpike
Hilarious adj.	funny, side splitting, extremely jovial, hysterical, gay
Hinder vb.	interrupt, hamper, slow, delay, obstruct, interfere with, block, thwart, prevent, stop

Hindrance n.	delay, interruption, obstruction, interference, barrier, obstacle, impediment
Hinge vb.	depend, rely, pivot
Hint n.	suggestion, tip, clue, suspicion, whisper **vb.** suggest mention
History n.	chronicle, annal, record, account, narrative, tale, memoir, story
Hit vb.	strike, smite, find, come upon, discover
Hitch vb.	tie, fasten, tether, harness **n.** hindrance, interruption, interference
Hoard vb.	amass, save, store, secrete **n.** store, stock, cache
Hoarse adj.	rough, raucous, deep, husky, grating, harsh
Hoary adj.	white, gray, old, ancient, venerable
Hobby n.	pastime, diversion, avocation
Hoist vb.	lift, raise, heave, elevate **n.** crane, derrick, elevator
Holdup n.	robbery **slang.** Heist, stick up, delay, slowdown, interruption
Hole n.	opening, tear, rip, aperture, burrow, pit, cave, den, lair
Holocaust n.	burning, fire, disaster, extermination, massacre, mass murder, butchery
Holy adj.	blessed, sacred, hallowed, consecrated, saintly, sainted, divine, pious

Homage n.	respect, reverence, honour
Homesick adj.	nostalgic, lonely
Homicide n.	murder, manslaughter, killing of a human being
Homogeneous adj.	of uniform structure, of one kind throughout, alike, same
Honest adj.	truthful, trustworthy, moral, upright, honourable, open, candid, forthright, frank, straightforward
Honour n.	respect, esteem, distinction, principle, character, honesty, uprightness
Hoodwink vb.	deceive, fool bamboozle, dupe
Hop n. vb.	leap, jump
Hope n.	expectation, anticipation, desire, trust, faith, confidence **vb.** desire, aspire, expect
Hopeful adj.	confident, optimistic
Hopeless adj.	despairing, desperate, forlorn, incurable, fatal, disastrous
Horde n.	multitude, crowd, mob, throng, host
Horrendous adj.	horrifying, horrible, horrid, awful, terrible, dreadful, ghastly
Horrible adj.	horrifying, awful, ghastly, terrible, horrid, horrendous
Horrid adj.	shocking, horrifying, horrible, revolting, repulsive
Horror n.	terror, dread, alarm, hatred, loathing, aversion
Horseplay n.	clowning, tomfoolery

Horticulture n.	gardening
Hospital n.	clinic, infirmary, sanatorium, rest home, nursing home
Hospitality n.	generosity, liberality, graciousness, warmth, welcome
Hostile adj.	unfriendly, antagonistic, warlike
Hostility n.	enmity, animosity, antagonism, hatred, unfriendliness, repugnance
Hotel n.	inn, motel, hostelry, hostel
Hotheaded adj.	reckless, rash, unruly, touchy, testy, irritable, short-tempered
Hound vb.	purse, harass, harry, pester
House n.	abode, building, dwelling, residence **vb.** shelter, lodge, harbor
Howl vb. n.	wail, yowl, cry, yell
Hue n.	colour, shade, tone, tint
Hug n. vb.	embrace, clasp, press, grasp
Huge adj.	enormous, gigantic, immense, big, colossal, tremendous, large
Humane adj.	kind, thoughtful, kindly, merciful, kindhearted, gentle, tender, softhearted
Humiliate vb.	degrade, disgrace, shame, humble
Humor n.	amusement, joking, clowning, fun, mood, sentiment, disposition
Humourous adj.	funny, comical, comic, amusing
Hungry adj.	famished, starved
Hurl vb.	fling, throw, pitch, cast

Hurry vb.	rush, run, speed, race, hasten, rush, hasten, urge, accelerate **n.** rush, haste, bustle, ado
Hurt vb.	damage, harm, injure, wound, distress, afflict, pain **n.** injury, harm, pain
Hush vb. n.	silence, quiet, still
Hush up vb. phr.	suppress, conceal, cover over, hide, keep secure, keep private
Hustle vb.	hurry, hasten, race, run, speed
Hut b.	cabin, cottage, shed, shanty
Hyperbole n.	exaggeration, excessive statement
Hypnotic adj.	mesmeric, soporific **n.** narcotic
Hypocrite adj.	formalist, deceiver, pretender
Hypothesis n.	supposition, theory, assumption, conjecture, unproved theory

I

Ideal n.	model, example, sample, paragon, standard, aim, objective, target, goal **adj.** perfect, complete, fitting supreme
Identical adj.	alike, indistinguishable, like, same
Identify vb.	name, describe, classify
Identity n.	individuality, character, uniqueness, personality
Ideology n.	belief, doctrine, credo, principles

Idle adj.	unemployed, inactive, unusual, unoccupied, lazy, sluggish
Idler n.	sluggard, lazy, indolent, laggard, slothful
Ignite vb.	kindle, take fire, set fire to, inflame, light
Ignore vb.	disregard, overlook, omit, neglect
Ill adj.	sick, unwell, unhealthy, diseased, ailing, indisposed
Ill-advised adj.	imprudent, injudicious, ill-considered
Ill-at-ease adj.	uneasy, uncomfortable, nervous
Illegal adj.	unlawful, illicit
Illicit adj.	illegal, unlawful, unauthorized
Illimitable adj.	boundless, infinite, endless, immeasurable, immense, vast
Illiterate adj.	uneducated, unlearned, unable to read and write, untaught, ignorant
Ill-mannered adj.	uncivil, discourteous, impolite, rude, unpolished, ill-behaved, uncouth
Illness n.	disease, sickness, indisposition, ailing, malady, ailment
Illogical adj.	irrational, absurd, preposterous
Ill-tempered adj.	ill-natured, cranky, crabby, cross, grouchy, irascible
Ill-treated adj.	abused, harmed, mistreated, maltreated
Illuminate vb.	light, light up, brighten, lighten, enlighten, explain, clarify, interpret

Illusion n.	mirage, delusion, hallucination, vision, fantasy, chimera
Illustrate vb.	illuminate, decorate, adorn, embellish, demonstrate, picture, show
Illustration n.	picture, photograph, example, explanation
Illustrator n.	artist, painter
Illustrious n.	famous, renowned, noted, prominent, famed, distinguished
Image n.	likeness, representation, reflection, idea, picture, notion, conception
Imaginary adj.	unreal, fanciful, whimsical, fantastic
Imaginative adj.	inventive, creative, fanciful, visionary, dreamy, poetic
Imagine vb.	conceive, picture, envisage, envision, suppose, believe, think
Imbibe vb.	assimilate, take in, absorb, acquire, gain, gather, pickup, acquire
Imitate vb.	follow, copy, mimic, duplicate, reproduce
Immaculate adj.	spotless, clean, unblemished
Immaterial adj.	unimportant, trivial, inconsequential, insignificant
Immature adj.	unprepared, unripe, unformed, untimely, crude, unfinished, undeveloped, youthful
Immediate adj.	instant, instantaneous, present, near, next, close, prompt, direct
Immediately adv.	at once, instantly, forthwith, directly, straight away, promptly

Immense adj.	huge, enormous, vast, gigantic, great, large, big
Immensity n.	enormousness, hugeness, vastness
Immerse vb.	dip, plunge, submerge, bathe, overwhelm, douse, sink, involve, engage, absorb
Imminent adj.	impending, overhanging, threatening, near at hand, dangerous, alarming
Immortal adj.	everlasting, eternal, timeless, endless
Immunity n.	freedom, exemption, release, exoneration, prerogative
Impact n.	contact, striking, collision
Impair vb.	mar, damage, spoil destroy
Impartial adj.	unbiased, just, equal, unprejudiced
Impasse n.	deadlock, standstill, stalemate
Impassioned adj.	passionate, vehement, impetuous, intense, ardent, animated, excited, fervent, zealous
Impatient adj.	restless, eager, impetuous, irritable, testy, fretful
Impede vb.	hinder, obstruct, stop, clog, retard, decay, interrupt, restrain, block, encumber, check
Impel vb.	push, urge, send, drive, put in motion, press on, urge forward, induce, move, persuade, influence, instigate, incite, actuate, stimulate, compel
Impending adj.	threatening, near at hand, imminent

Imperfection n.	flaw, blemish, defect
Imperil vb.	endanger, jeopardize, risk
Impersonal adj.	detached, objective, disinterested, impassioned
Impertinence n.	rudeness, impudence, insolence, incivility
Impertinent adj.	impudent, insolent, rude, disrespectful
Impetuous adj.	rash, hasty, impulsive
Implement n.	tool, untensil, instrument, device **vb.** complete, fulfill, achieve, realise
Implicate vb.	incriminate, involve
Implore vb.	beg, beseech, entreat
Imply vb.	hint, suggest, indicate, mention
Impolite adj.	rude, unpleasant, insolent, discourteous, impertinent, discourteous, impertinent, uncivil
Impose vb.	required, levy, demand
Imposing adj.	impressive, majestic, grand, stately
Imposition n.	burden, onus, load
Impostor n.	deceive, pretender, cheat, rogue, counterfeiter
Impossible adj.	unassailable, secure, safe, invulnerable, invincible
Impress vb.	influence, affect, awe, indent, emboss, mark, imprint, print
Impression n.	effect, mark, influence, mark, dent, indentation, depression, thought, belief, guess, opinion

Impressive adj.	effective, affecting, splendid, moving, striking, emphatic, stirring
Imprint vb.	print, stamp, mark by pressure, impress, inculcate, fix deeply
Impromptu adj.	off-the-cuff, casual, offhand, extemporaneous, unprepared
Improper adj.	unsuitable, unfit, inappropriate, indecent, naughty, unbecoming
Impropriety n.	unsuitableness, unfitness, inappropriateness
Improve vb.	better, refine, upgrade, mend
Imprudent adj.	indiscreet, ill-advised, thoughtless, irresponsible
Impudent adj.	impertinent, fresh, insolent, insulting, rude
Impulse n.	whim, hunch, fancy, caprice, urge, force, surge, pulse
Impulsive adj.	hasty, rash, spontaneous, automatic
Inaccessible adj.	unapproachable, unattainable
Inaccurate adj.	incorrect, wrong, mistaken, faulty
Inactive adj.	inert, motionless, still, idle
Inadvertent adj.	negligent, careless, unthinking, thoughtless
Inane adj.	silly, stupid, absurd, foolish
Inanimate adj.	lifeless, mineral, vegetable
Inaugurate vb.	initiate, launch, open, start, begin, commence
Inborn adj.	innate, inherent inbred, natural, instinctive, congenital, ingrained

In brief adj. phr.	in short, concisely, briefly, in a nutshell
Incapability n.	incapacity, inability, incompetence, disability
Incense vb.	enrage, infuriate, anger
Incentive n.	inducement, stimulus, impulse, encouragement
Incessant adj.	unending, eternal, continuous, perpetual, constant, relentless
Incident n.	event, occurrence, happening
Incidental adj.	secondary, unimportant, trivial, accidental, casual
Incidentally adv.	by the way, by the by
Inclement adj.	severe, rigorous, harsh, boisterous, stormy, cruel, destitute of clemency
Inclination n.	tendency, predisposition, preference, prejudice, slope, slant, incline, lean
Incline vb.	lean, slope, nod
Include vb.	embrace, encompass, contain, involve
Income n.	salary, earning, wages, pay, revenue, receipts, return
Incomparable adj.	matchless, peerless, unequaled
Incongruous adj.	inconsistent, unfit, inappropriate, absurd, unsuitable, contradictory
Inconsiderate adj.	unthoughtful, unthinking, thoughtless, unmindful, careful

Inconsistent adj.	illogical, self-contradictory, contradictory
Inconspicuous adj.	unnotice, retiring, unostentatious
Inconvenient adj.	inappropriate, awkward, troublesome, untimely
Incorrect adj.	wrong, inaccurate, mistaken, erroneous
Incredible adj.	unbelievable, improbable
Incriminate vb.	accuse, charge, blame, impeach, criminate
Incriminate vb.	accuse, charge, blame, impeach, criminate
Inculcate vb.	impress, enforce, instill, infuse, inspire, implant
Indecent adj.	improper, unbecoming, outrageous, immodest, shameless, indecorous, gross, indelicate
Indeed adv.	really, in fact, truthfully, surely, honestly
Indefinite adj.	uncertain, unsure, vague, unsettled, confused, confusing
Indelible adj.	ingrained, fixed, fast, permanent, not to be blotted out, ineffaceable
Indemnify vb.	secure, guarantee, compensate, reimburse, requite
Independence vb.	liberty, freedom
Indicate vb.	signify, symbolize, mean, point out, show, designate

Indifferent adj.	unconcerned, uncaring, cool, insensitive, nonchalant
Indigenous adj.	native, home-grown, aboriginal
Indigent adj.	poor, destitute, needy, insolvent, necessitous
Indignant adj.	angry, irritated, aroused, exasperated, irate
Indignity n.	insult, affront, outrage, slight, disrespect, dishonor
Indirect adj.	roundabout, circuitous
Indistinct adj.	vague, blurred, blurry, hazy
Individual adj.	single, undivided, separate, apart, different, distinct, special **n.** person, human, human being
Indolent adj.	lazy, idle, slow, sluggish, inactive
Induce vb.	persuade, influence, convince
Inducement n.	lure, enticement, incentive, stimulus
Induct vb.	instill, initate, introduce, establish
Indulge vb.	yield to, gratify, humor, satisfy
Indulgent adj.	tolerant, easy, obliging, pampering
Industrious adj.	hard-working, busy, diligent, persistent
Inebriated adj.	drunk, intoxicated, soused, sizzled, drunken, besotted, gorged **n.** drunkard, sob, boozer, toper, wino, alcoholic
In effect n. phr.	in fact, in truth, in reality, really
Inert adj.	motionless, unmoving, fixed, static, immobile, lifeless, inanimate

Inevitable adj.	unavoidable, inescapable, sure, certain
Inexpensive adj.	how-priced, modest, economical, cheap
Infamous adj.	scandalous, shocking, shameful, wicked, evil, bad
Infantile adj.	childish, immature, babyish, naïve
Infatuated adj.	besotted, captivated
Infectious adj.	catching, communicable, contagious, transferable
Infer vb.	deduce, extract, understand
Inferior adj.	lower, second-rate, mediocre
Inflame vb.	excite, arouse, incite, fire
Inflammation n.	irritation, soreness, infection
Inflammatory adj.	provocative, inciting, rabble-rousing, instigating
Inflate vb.	swell, expand, blow up, distend
Inflexible adj.	rigid, unbending, firm, unyielding, immovable, steadfast
Inflict vb.	give, deliver, deal, impose, levy, apply
Influence n.	effect, sway, weight, control **vb.** affect, control, sway, impress
Inform vb.	notify, advise, tell, relate
Information n.	facts, data, knowledge, intelligence
Informative adj.	enlightening, instructive, educational
Informer n.	betrayer, traitor, tattler, rat
Infringe vb.	break, violate, transgress, encroach, upon, trespass, intrude, trench, upon

Ingenious adj.	resourceful, imaginative, inventive, creative
Ingenuous adj.	naive, simple, innocent, unsophisticated
Ingredient n.	element, component, constituent
Inhabit vb.	occupy, live, dwell or reside in
Inherent adj.	innate, natural, inborn, inbred, ingrained, instrinsic
Inheritance n.	heritage, legacy, patrimony
Inhibit vb.	curb, repress, control, restrain
Inhuman adj.	barbaric, savage, brutal, bestial
Initial adj.	first, basic, primary, elementary
Initiate vb.	first, begin, commence, open
Initiative n.	enterprise, enthusiasm, energy, vigour
Injure vb.	harm, damage, hurt, wound
Injurious adj.	harmful, hurtful, damaging, destructive
Injury n.	harm, damage, hurt, wound
Inmate n.	prisoner, patient
Inn n.	hotel, lodge, motel
Innocent adj.	not guilty, blameless, faultless, virtuous, naïve, unknowing, unsophisticated
Innovate vb.	introduce novelties, make changes, invent
Innuendo n.	insinuation, oblique hint, sly suggestion
Inquire vb.	ask, question, investigate, examine

Inquiry n.	examination, study, inquiry, search, investigation, examination
Inquisition n.	inquest, judicial, inquiry, search, investigation, examination
Inquisitive adj.	inquiring, questioning, praying, curious
Insane adj.	deranged, lunatic, demented, mentally unsound, crazy, mad, senseless, foolish, stupid, idiotic
Insecure adj.	shaky, nervous, uneasy, uncertain
Insensitive adj.	callous, hard, tough, unfeeling
Insincere adj.	deceitful, dishonest, false
Insidious adj.	artful, crafty, cunning, subtle, deceitful, diplomatic, crooked, deceptive
Insinuate vb.	suggest, indirectly, hint or suggest remotely
Insipid adj.	tasteless, vapid, flat, lifeless, dull, spiritless
Insist vb.	demand, require, command
Insolent adj.	impertinent, rude, disrespectful, insulting
Insomnia n.	sleeplessness, indisposition to sleep, inability to sleep
Inspect vb.	examine, investigate
Inspiration n.	thought, impulse, idea, notion, hunch
Install vb.	establish, set up, put in
Instant n.	moment, flash, twinkling

Instantly adv.	at once, immediately, right away, directly, instantaneously
Instinct n.	feeling, intuition, impulse
Institute vb.	establish, organize, found, launch, begin, initiate **n.** establishment, organization, university
Instruct vb.	teach, educate, train, tutor, school, drill, order, direct, command
Instruction n.	training, teaching, educating, schooling, guidance, order, direction, command
Instrument n.	tool, implement, device, means
Insult vb.	offend, outrage, humiliate **n.** offense, affront, outrage, scorn
Integral adj.	whole, entire, total, complete, necessary for completeness
Integrated adj.	combined, interspersed, mingled, mixed, desegregated, interracial, nonsectarian
Integrity n.	soundness, wholeness, honesty, uprightness, honour, virtue, principle
Intellect n.	judgment, understanding, intelligence, mind, mentality, sense, reason, hrains
Intellectual adj.	intelligent, learned **n.** academic, scholar, academician
Intelligence n.	ability, skill, aptitude
Intelligent adj.	smart, bright, clever, quick, astute, alert, wise

Intend vb.	mean, expert, plan, propose
Intent n.	aim, purpose, intention **adj.** concentrated, set, steadfast
Intension n.	plan, intent, purpose, design, aim, expectation, object
Intentional adv.	purposeful, deliberate, planned, intended
Intentionally adj.	purposefully, on purpose, deliberately, maliciously
Intercede vb.	mediate, arbitrate, interpose, plead, make intercession
Intercept vb.	stop on the way, seize on the passing, interrupt, cut off, obstruct
Interchangeably adv.	alternately, by interchange, by reciprocation
Intercourse n.	communication, dealings, converse, mutual exchange
Interested adj.	concerned, involve, affected
Interesting adj.	attractive, fascinating, engaging, inviting
Interfere vb.	meddle, butt in, intervene
Interference n.	meddling, intrusion, prying, obstruction, obstacle, barrier
Interim n.	interval, intermediate time, meantime
Interior n.	insider, center **adj.** inside, central, inner, internal
Interlace vb.	intertwine, twist, plait, mix, intersperse, unite, blind

Interlope n.	meddler, intruder
Internal adj.	inner, interior, inside, private, intimate, domestic, native
Internecine adj.	mortal, deadly, exterminating, mutually destructive
Interpret vb.	explain, define, understand, translate, paraphrase
Interrupt vb.	intrude, break in, cut in (on), interfere, discontinue, stop, hinder, obstruct
Interval n.	gap, pause
Intervene vb.	come, between, interfere, interrupt, intrude
Intimidate vb.	frighten, scare, terrorize, bully, terrify, subdue, daunt
Intolerant adj.	prejudiced, biased, bigoted
In toto *l.*	wholly, entirely, intoxicated **adj.** drunk, inebriated
Intrepid adj.	bold, fearless, undaunted, valiant, courageous, daring, gallant, valorous
Intrigue vb.	attract, charm, interest, captivate **n.** plot, scheme, conspiracy
Intrinsic adj.	inherent, inborn, inbred, ingrained, natural, real, genuine, true, essential
Introduce vb.	present, acquaint, submit, propose, present, offer
Intrude vb.	interrupt, infringe
Intruder n.	prowler, thief, trespasser, robber
Intuition vb.	instinct, sixth sense, insight, clairvoyance

Intumesce vb.	swell, expand, dilate, bubble up, become tumid
Inure vb.	habituate, accustom, use, train, familiarise, toughen, harden, discipline
Invade vb.	penetrate
Invaluable adj.	valuable, precious, priceless
Invasion n.	intrusion, attack
Inveigle vb.	entice, cajole, ensnare, lure, beguile
Invent vb.	create, make up, originate, devise, contrive
Investigate vb.	examine, inspect, explore, study
Invigorating adj.	stimulating, vitalizing, bracing, fortifying
Invite vb.	ask, bid, request, encourage, urge
Inviting adj.	alluring, luring, appealing, tempting, attractive, encouraging
In vogue adj. phr.	fashionable, in fashion, the rage
Invoke vb.	implore, supplicate, beseech, entreat, solicit, appeal to
Involuntary adj.	automatic, reflex, uncontrolled, unintentional
Involve vb.	include, contain, embrace, complicate, confuse, entangle
Iota n.	jot, bit, grain, scrap, trace, glimmer, particle, atom
Irate adj.	angry, furious, enraged, incensed
Ire n.	anger, rage, wrath, fury, indignation, resentment

Irk vb.	annoy, irritate, provoke, vex
Irony n.	mockery, sarcasm
Irregular adj.	uneven, unequal, crooked, disorderly, random, unsettled, disorganized
Irresponsible adj.	untrustworthy, unreliable
Irritate vb.	annoy, vex, pester, bother, redden, chafe, inflame
Irritable adj.	sensitive, touchy testy, peevish, short-tempered
Isolate vb.	separate, disconnect, detach, segregate
Isolation n.	separation, segregation, detachment, solitude, loneliness
Itemize vb.	list, record, detail, register
Itinerary n.	route, circuit

J

Jabber vb.	chatter, gabble, talk, rapidly, talk idly
Jackass n.	idiot, fool, dope, dunce, imbecile, simpleton, ignoramus, jerk, ninny, nincompoop, blockhead
Jail n.	prison, penitentiary, reformatory, stockade, brig, dungeon, keep **vb.** imprison, confine, detain, lock up, incarcerate
Jailer vb.	keeper, guard, warden, turnkey

Jam vb.	pack, crowd, force, ram, push, squeeze, wedge **n.** preserve, conserve
Jargon n.	vernacular, argot, parlance, patois
Jaundiced adj.	prejudiced, biased
Jaunty adj.	airy, showy, finical, fluttering, sprightly, unconcerned
Jealous adj.	envious, covetous
Jealousy n.	envy, covetousness, greed
Jeopardy n.	hazard, endanger, peril, risk, venture
Jeoparadise vb.	endanger, imperil, risk
Jerk vb.	twitch, quiver, shake **n.** twitch, spasm, shake, quiver, fool dope
Jet n.	spurt, squirt
Job n.	work, employment, trade, profession, position, career, calling, business, task, chore, duty
Join vb.	untie, connect, couple, assemble, link, fit, attach
Jocund adj.	joyous, joyful, merry, cheerful, blithe, sportive, jolly, playful, lively, gay, debonair
Joint n.	connection, link, coupling, union, junction **adj.** common, mutual, combined, connected
Joke n.	prank, game, caper, antic, jest, anecdote **vb.** jest, banter, laugh
Jolly adj.	joyful, gleeful, gay, spirited, happy, cheerful, glad

Jolt vb. n.	jar, bump, bounce, shake, shock
Journal n.	dairy, account, record, newspaper, daily
Journey n.	trip, voyage, excursion, tour **vb.** travel
Joy n.	delight, pleasure, happiness, gladness, satisfaction
Judgment n.	decision, verdict, estimation, opinion, understanding, wisdom, discretion, sense, common sense, intelligence
Jug n.	jar, bottle, flagon, flask, pitcher
Jump vb. n.	leap, spring, bound, vault, skip, hop
Jumpy adj.	nervous, touchy, sensitive, excitable
Junction n.	joining, coupling, union, intersection, crossroads, connection, joint, weld, seam
Junta n.	cabal, faction, party, gag, secret, council
Jurisdiction n.	extent of authority, legal power, authority, sphere, range, reach, control, judicature
Just adj.	fair, impartial, rightful, lawful, legal, proper
Justify vb.	vindicate, clear, acquit, excuse, defend, explain, excuse
Juvenile adj.	childish, puerile, immature, young, babyish **n.** youngster, child, teenager, youth
Juxtaposition n.	proximity, contact, contiguity, adjacency

K

Keen adj.	sharp, acute, quick, shrewd, bright, clever, intelligent, enthusiastic, eager, interested
Keep vb.	retain, hold, withhold, preserve, maintain, continue, persist in, save, store, hold **n.** room and board, maintenance, subsistence, tower, dungeon
Keep back vb. phr.	delay, hinder, hold, check
Keep dark vb. phr.	be secretive, keep the matter to one's self, seal the lips
Keep on vb. phr.	continue, persist in, endure
Keep vb. phr.	maintain, sustain, support
Keeper n.	jailer, warden, custodian, guard
Keepsake n.	memento, souvenir, remembrance
Kernel n.	core, heart, nucleus
Key n.	clue, answer
Kick up dust vb. phr.	make a commotion, create an excitement, make a stir
Killing n.	slaughter, massacre, butchery, genocide, carnage, bloodshed
Kind n.	sort, class, type, variety
Kind adj.	friendly, gentle, kindly, mild, kindhearted, goodhearted, warm, tender, affectionate

Kindle vb.	ignite, fire, light, execute, arouse, inflame, provoke
Kindly adj.	kind, warm, warmhearted, kindhearted
Kingdom n.	monarchy, realm, domain, empire
Kingly adj.	regal, kinglike, royal, majestic, imperial
Kit n.	set, collection, outfit
Knack n.	talent, skill, aptitude, ability
Knit vb.	combine, join, mend, unite, heal
Knob n.	handle, doorknob, bump, protuberance
Knock vb. n.	rap, thump, whack, thwack, tap
Knot n.	group, cluster, collection, gathering, crowd, tangle, twist, snarl
Know vb.	recognize, understand, see, comprehend, distinguish, discriminate
Knowing adj.	smart, sage, sagacious, wise, shrewd, clever
Knowledge n.	information, learning, data, understanding, wisdom, judgment
Knuckle vb.	yield, submit, stoop, give up, crouch, cringe
Kudos n.	praise, acclaim, approval, approbation

L

Label n.	tag, marker, mark, sticker, stamp **vb.** tag, mark, stamp
Labour n.	work, toil, drudgery, workingmen, workers, working, class **vb.** work, toil, strive
Labourious adj.	difficult, tiring, burdensome, hard, painstaking, industrious
Lack n.	shortage, need, dearth, want, scarcity **vb.** want, need, require
Lad n.	boy, youth, fellow, chap, stripling
Lame adj.	crippled, disabled, limping, deformed, poor, unsatisfactory, weak, inadequate, faulty
Lament vb.	mourn, weep, bemoan, grieve, regret **n.** mourning, lamentation, moan, wail, moaning, wailing, weeping
Lamentable adj.	deplorable, unfortunate
Lane n.	passage, alley, way
Language n.	tongue, speech, dialect, jargon, patois
Lank adj.	lean, gaunt, slender, thin
Large adj.	big, great, sizable, broad, massive, huge, vast, enormous, immense
Largely adv.	mainly, chiefly, mostly, principally
Largesse n.	bounty, present, donation, gift, endowment, grant, bequest
Lark n.	frolic, fling, sport, play

Lash n.	ship, thong, cane, rod, knout **vb.** hit, whip
Lass n.	girl, maiden, damsel
Lastly adv.	recently, of late
Lather n.	foam, suds, froth
Latitude n.	freedom, scope, range, extent
Laud vb.	praise, extol, celebrate, admire, commend, magnify
Laudable adj.	praiseworthy, admirable, creditable, commendable
Laugh vb. n.	chuckle, giggle, snicker, guffaw
Laughable adj.	amusing, funny, humorous, comical, ridiculous
Laughing stock n.	object of ridicule
Launch vb.	fire, drive, propel, initiate, originate, start, begin
Law n.	rule, statute, order, decree, ruling
Lawful adj.	legal, legitimate
Lawless adj.	uncontrolled, uncivilized, wild, untamed, savage, violent
Lawyer n.	attorney, counsel, counselor, advocate, counselor-at-law
Lax adj.	loose, relaxed, slack, negligent, neglectful
Layout n.	arrangement, plan, design
Lazy adj.	indolent, slothful, idle, inactive, sluggish
Lead vb.	guide, conduct, direct, steer, command, direct

Leader n.	director, chief, commander, head, manager, ruler
League n.	alliance, union, combination
Leagued adj.	untied, combined, allied, banded, confederate
Leak vb.	drip, flow
Lean vb.	slant, tilt, slope, rely, depend, trust
Leap vb. n.	jump, vault, spring, bound
Learn vb.	acquire, gain, determine, find out, memorize
Learn by heart vb. phr.	memorise, commit to memory learn or get by rote
Learned adj.	scholarly, wise, educated, knowledgeable, well-informed
Learning n.	knowledge, lore, scholarship, education
Lease vb.	rent, charter, let
Least adj.	smallest, tiniest, minutest, slightest, trivial
Left n.	sinistral, sinistrous, (nautical) port
Leftovers n. pl.	remains, scarps, remainder, residue
Legacy n.	inheritance, bequest
Legal adj.	lawful, legitimate, honest
Legate n.	agent, emissary, envoy, representative
Legend n.	story, myth, tale, fable, folk tale
Legendary adj.	traditional, mythical, fictitious, fanciful, imaginary

Legitimate adj.	legal, lawful, right, proper, correct, valid
Leisure n.	relaxation, ease, recreation, rest
Leisurely adj.	unhurried, casual, relaxed, comfortable
Lend vb.	loan, advance
Length n.	extent, measure, reach, stretch, longness
Lengthen vb.	extend, stretch, reach, prolong, grow, increase
Lessen vb.	reduce, diminish, decline
Lesson n.	exercise, drill, assignment, homework, instruction
Let vb.	permit, allow, grant, lease, rent
Letdown n.	disappointment, disillusionment
Lethal adj.	deadly, mortal, fatal
Lethargic adj.	slow, sluggish, lazy, logy, listless, phlegmatic
Letup n.	lessening, slackening, slowdown, reduction, abatement
Level-headed adj.	sensible, reasonable, collected, calm, cool
Levy n.	tax, charge, toll, duty
Lexicon n.	dictionary, glossary, vocabulary, word-book
Liable adj.	subject, accountable, answerable, responsible
Liaison n.	relation, connection, union, illicit, intimacy, amour, intrigue

Liar n.	falsifier, prevaricator, fibber, fabricator
Liberate vb.	free, release, loose, deliver
Liberty n.	freedom, independence
Lid n.	cover, top, cap
Lie n.	falsehood, fib, untruth, fiction, prevarication, perjury
Lie vb.	recline, repose, be situated or located **n.** situation, location, site
Lift vb.	raise, elevate
Light-fingered adj.	thievish
Light-hearted adj.	gay, carefree, careful, merry, happy, glad
Like vb.	admire, esteem, fancy, care for, cherish, adore, love
Likely adj.	provable, liable, possible, reasonable
Likeness n.	resemblance, similarity, image, representation, picture, portrait
Likewise adv.	similarly, besides, also
Liking n.	affection, partiality, fondness
Limpid adj.	clear, lucid, pure, bright, transparent, crystal, clear, translucent
Linger vb.	loiter, stay, remain, terry, dawdle
Lion-hearted adj.	brave, courageous, intrepid, dauntless
List n.	roll, record
State vb.	record, register, post, file
Listen vb.	hear, attend

Listless adj.	lethargic, spiritless
Literal adj.	word for word, verbatim, exact
Literate adj.	educated, informed, intelligent
Litter n.	trash, rubbish **vb.** strew, scatter
Live vb.	abide, reside, dwell
Live adj.	alive, surviving, energetic, active
Lively adj.	active, live, vigorous, animated, spirited
Livelihood n.	maintenance, sustenance, subsistence, living
Livid adj.	extremely angry
Living n.	livelihood
Load n.	burden **vb.** weight, burden
Loan n.	advance, credit **vb.** lend, advance
Loathsome adj.	abominable, hateful, atrocious
Lobby n.	vestibule, foyer, anteroom
Locate vb.	find, discover
Location n.	site, situation, locale
Lock[1] n.	tress, braid, plait
Lock[2] n.	latch, hasp, bolt, padlock **vb.** latch, padlock, bolt, fasten
Lodge n.	cottage, cabin **vb.** room, reside, abide
Lodger n.	tenant, occupant, boarder
Lofty adj.	high, towering, exalted, elevated, proud
Logical adj.	reasonable, rational, sensible
Lone adj.	sole, alone, solitary

Lonely adj.	lonesome, alone
Lonesome adj.	alone, lone, remote, secluded, barren, desolate
Long adj.	extensive, length, extended
Long vb.	crave, desire, wish
Long for vb. phr.	crave for, pine for, yearn for, aspire for
Longstanding adj.	established, persistent
Long-suffering adj.	patient, enduring, forbearing **n.** forbearance
Long-winded adj.	dull, boring
Loose adj.	unfastened, baggy **vb.** loosen, set free
Loosen vb.	untie, undo, unchain, unfasten
Loot n.	plunder, booty **vb.** rob, steal, plunder
Lopsided adj.	uneven, unequal, distorted, twisted
Loquacious adj.	talkative, garrulous
Lose vb.	misplace
Lose ground vb. phr.	decline, lose credit
Lost adj.	missing, misplaced
Lotion n.	balm, cream
Loud adj.	noisy, thunderous, blaring
Lounge vb.	idle, laze **n.** couch, sofa, divan, davenport
Love n.	adoration warmth, liking, affection **vb.** adore, treasure, cherish, like

Lovely adj.	attractive, fair, beautiful, handsome
Lower vb.	reduce, decrease, diminish, degrade
Lowly adj.	humble, lowborn
Loyal adj.	faithful, true, devoted, dependable
Loyalty n.	faithfulness, devotion, fidelity, allegiance
Lucid adj.	clear, crystal-clear, transparent
Luck n.	fortune, chance
Lucky adj.	fortunate, favoured, favourable, blessed
Lucrative adj.	profitable, well-paying, high-paying, money-making
Luggage n.	baggage
Lugubrious adj.	mournful, somber, gloomy, melancholy
Lukewarm adj.	tepid, unenthusiastic
Lull vb.	calm, soothe **n.** calm, hush, quiet, stillness, silence
Luminous adj.	light, glowing, bright, fluorescent
Lump n.	bump, protuberance
Lump n.	bump, protuberance
Lupine adj.	wolfish, ravenous
Lure n.	attraction, temptation **vb.** entice, attract, tempt
Luscious adj.	juicy, delicious
Lust n.	desire, passion, craving, lechery, wantonness
Luxuriant adj.	lush, dense, rich, splendid

M

Macabre adj.	gruesome, horrible, ghastly, grim
Machiavellian adj.	artful, cunning, deceitful, shrewd
Machine n.	device, contrivance, motor, mechanism
Mad adj.	insane, crazy, deranged, angry, furious, raging
Madden vb.	infuriate, anger, vex, annoy
Magazine n.	periodical, journal, arsenal, armory
Magic n.	sorcery **adj.** magical
Magical adj.	marvellous, miraculous, mystical
Magician n.	sorcerer, wizard, conjuror
Magnanimous adj.	noble, generous, exalted, honorable
Magnate n.	nobleman, man of rank
Magnetism n.	attraction, appeal, allure
Magnificence n.	splendor, grandeur, luxury
Magnify vb.	enlarge, increase
Magnitude n.	extent, dimension, significance
Maiden adj.	first, original, foremost
Maintain vb.	continue, keep up, preserve
Maintenance n.	support, living, subsistence
Majestic adj.	royal, kingly, princely, regal
Majesty n.	dignity, nobility, grandeur
Major adj.	greater, larger, important, chief
Make believe vb. phr.	pretend, fantasize, imagine

Make good vb. phr.	compensate, reimburse
Make it vb. phr.	succeed, trumph
Make shift n.	substitute, temporary, expedient
Make sport of vb. phr.	mock, ridicule, deride, scoff at, jeer, at, laugh at
Make up vb. phr.	invent, fabricate, compose
Makeup n.	cosmetics
Maladroit adj.	awkward, clumsy, inapt
Malady n.	illness, sickness, affliction, disorder
Male adj.	masculine, manly, virile
Malice n.	spite, resentment, bitterness
Malign adj.	malicious, malignant **vb.** disparage, scandalise, slander
Malignant adj.	deadly, fatal, terminal, lethal
Mammoth adj.	huge, colossal, gigantic
Manage vb.	direct, guide, lead, supervise, superintend, control, manipulate
Management n.	control, regulation, administration
Manager n.	supervisor, superintendent, overseer, executive
Mandate n.	command, order
Mandatory adj.	required, obligatory, compulsory
Manifest n.	evident **vb.** show, exhibit, reveal, disclose, prove, expose
Manly adj.	masculine, manful
Manner n.	way, method, style
Mannerism n.	peculiarity

Manufacture vb.	make, assemble, fabricate, construct
Map n. vb.	chart, graph
Margin n.	edge, rim, border
Marginal adj.	borderline
Marine adj.	maritime, oceanic, nautical
Mariner n.	sailor, seaman
Mark n.	impression, effect, imprint, brand, sign **vb.** label, tag, price, ticket
Mark down vb. phr.	reduce or cut (a price)
Mark off vb. phr.	separate, segregate, designate
Mark up vb. phr.	increase or raise (a price)
Market n.	marketplace, bazaar, stall **vb.** sell, merchandise
Marriage n.	wedding, nuptials, matrimony, wedlock, union
Marry vb.	wed, betroth
Marsh n.	swamp, quagmire
Marshal vb.	arrange, order, organise, rank
Marvel adj.	wonder, miracle, phenomenon **vb.** wonder, stare, gape
Mask n.	disguise, camouflage **vb.** conceal, hide, disguise, veil
Masquerade n.	mask, revel, disguise, mask, veil, cover
Mass n.	pile, heap, quantity **vb.** gather, amass, accumulate, collect, marshal
Massacre n.	slaughter, genocide **vb.** slay, murder, kill, butcher, exterminate

Massive adj.	huge, immense, gigantic, tremendous, large
Mast n.	spar, pole, post
Masterful adj.	commanding, dictatorial
Masterly adj.	skilful, expert, superb, adroit
Mastermind n.	genius, expert **vb.** manage, direct
Masterpiece n.	masterwork
Match n.	equal, equivalent, peer, rivalry, contest
Matchless adj.	unequalled, unrivalled, incomparable
Mate n.	associate, companion
Matter n.	substance, material, affair, subject
Matter-of-fact n. phr.	fact, reality, actuality
Meadow n.	pasture, field, plain
Meager adj.	sparse, insignificant
Meal n.	refreshment, breakfast, lunch, dinner
Mean vb.	intend, plan, expect, denote, signify, say, express, suggest
Mean adj.	unkind, cruel, nasty
Mean n.	average
Meander n.	labyrinth, maze, run in a serpentine
Meaning n.	sense, signification, significance, gist
Meaningless adj.	senseless, nonsensical, unreasonable
Means n. pl.	wealth, riches, money, resources
Measure n.	extent, size, weight, volume, bulk, dimension **vb.** rule, weigh
Measureless adj.	limitless, measurable, boundless, vast, infinite

Meat n.	flesh, food
Mechanic n.	machinist, repairman
Mechanism n.	machine, machinery, device, tool, contrivance
Medal n.	award, reward
Meddle vb.	interfere, pry
Mediate vb.	interpose, arbitrate, intercede **adj.** middle, interposed, intervening
Medicine n.	medication, drug, remedy
Mediocre adj.	ordinary, commonplace, average
Medley n.	mixture, jumble, miscellany
Meet vb.	encounter, gather, assemble
Melancholy n.	sadness, gloom, depression **adj.** downcast
Mellow adj.	ripe, mature, cured, sweet, melodious **vb.** ripen, mature, develop
Melody n.	tune, music, song
Melt vb.	liquefy, dissolve
Memorable adj.	historic
Memory n.	recollection, remembrance
Menace n.	threat, warning
Mend vb.	repair, patch, fix, improve, recover, recuperate, heal
Mendacity n.	duplicity, deception, deceit
Mental adj.	reasoning, intellectual, thinking
Mercenary adj.	greedy, covetous, money, grasping
Merchandise n.	wares, stock, commodities
Merchant n.	retailer, trader, dealer, businessman
Merciless adj.	cruel, ruthless

Mercurial adj.	inconstant, changeable, fickle
Mercy n.	compassion, sympathy, tenderness
Merge vb.	immerse, involve, submerge
Merit n.	worth, value, worthiness **vb.** be worthy of
Merry adj.	cheerful, joyous, jovial
Mess n.	untidiness, dirtiness, disorder, confusion, muddle **vb.** confuse, muddle, dirty
Message n.	communication, letter, memorandum, memo
Messenger n.	courier, bearer
Messy adj.	dirty, disorderly
Method n.	way, technique, manner, approach, means
Middle n.	centre, midpoint
Middleman n.	agent, broker, dealer, representative, intermediary, go-between
Midst n.	middle, centre, heart
Might n.	power, strength, force
Mighty adj.	strong, powerful
Migrate vb.	immigrate, emigrate
Migratory n.	wandering, roving, unsettled
Mild adj.	calm, gentle, temperate, amiable, calm, bland, soothing
Mind n.	intelligent, brain, intelligence **vb.** care for, look after
Mindful adj.	open-eyed, alert, watchful

Mine n.	pit, shaft, excavation **vb.** dig, excavate, drill, quarry
Mingle vb.	combine, mix, blend
Miniature adj.	tiny, small, little, minute
Minimise vb.	diminish, decrease
Minor adj.	smaller, secondary, petty, unimportant **n.** boy, girl, child, youth, adolescent
Mint vb.	coin, punch, stamp
Miraculous adj.	marvellous, wonderful, extraordinary
Mirror n.	looking-glass, glass, reflector
Mirth n.	glee, joy, gaiety, joyousness, merriment
Miscarry vb.	fail, go wrong
Miscellaneous adj.	various, mixed, mingled, heterogeneous
Mischievous adj.	playful, naughty
Misconstrue vb.	misinterpret, misjudge, misunderstand, misapprehend
Miser n.	scrooge
Miserable adj.	unhappy, wretched, poverty stricken, unlucky, unfortunate
Misery adj.	stingy, tightfisted, mean
Misery n.	unhappiness, suffering, anguish, woe, agony, distress
Misgiving n.	doubt, hesitation, mistrust, uncertainty
Misguided adj.	misled, misdirected
Mislay vb.	lose, misplace
Mismatched adj.	unsuitable, unsuited, incompatible

Misnomer n.	misnaming
Miss vb.	want, desire, crave, yearn for **n.** slip, failure, error, blunder
Missile n.	projectile, shot
Mist n.	fog, cloud, haze, steam
Mistake n.	error, slip, fault **vb.** misunderstand, misjudge, confuse, misinterpret
Mistaken adj.	confused, misinformed, inaccurate
Mistreat vb.	abuse, maltreat
Misunderstand vb.	misinterpret, misjudge, confuse
Mitigate vb.	appease, soothe, soften, mollify, pacify, quell, diminish
Mix vb.	combine, blend, mingle **n.** blend, mixture
Mixture n.	mix, confusion, blend
Moan n. vb.	groan, wail, lament, cry
Mob n.	swarm, crowd, rabble
Mobile adj.	movable, free, portable
Mock vb.	scorn, deride, ridicule **adj.** fraudulent, sham
Mockery n.	ridicule, scorn, travesty, sham
Mode n.	manner, method
Model n.	pattern, mold
Moderate[1] adj.	reasonable, average, cautious
Modern adj.	present-day, up to date, recent
Modernize vb.	refurbish, refurnish, rebuild, improve, renew, renovate

Modest adj.	demure, decent, humble, simple, plain
Modesty n.	humility, simplicity, decency, propriety
Modicum n.	little, trifle, small
Modify vb.	change, alter, change, curb
Moist adj.	damp, dark, humid, clammy, wet
Moisten vb.	dampen, wet
Moisture n.	dampness, wetness
Moment n.	instant, flash
Monarch n.	king, ruler, emperor, empress, sovereign
Money n.	coin, cash, currency, bills, notes
Monitor n.	supervisor, director, advisor **vb.** watch, observe, control, supervise
Monotone n.	sameness or uniformity of tone, monotony
Monotonous adj.	boring, dull, tedious, humdrum
Monster n.	beast, fiend, villain, wretch, demon
Mood n.	temper, humour, disposition
Moody adj.	temperamental, changeable, irritable
Moral adj.	honest, just, good
Morale n.	spirit, confidence
Moreover adv.	also, further, furthermore, in addition, besides
Morsel n.	bite, tidbit, bit, piece
Mortal adj.	human, perishable, momentary, deadly

Mortified adj.	humiliated, embarrassed, ashamed
Mostly adv.	generally, chiefly, mainly, largely, principally
Motherly adj.	maternal, like a mother
Motion n.	movement, change **vb.** gesture, signal, indicate
Motivate vb.	stimulate
Motive n.	reason, purpose, idea, cause, ground
Mottled adj.	motley, speckled, dappled, variegated
Motto n.	slogan, byword, catchword, saying
Mound n.	hill, hillock, pile, heap
Mount vb.	ascend, climb, go up, rise, increase, ascend
Mountain n.	mount, alp, peak, ridge, range
Mourn vb.	lament, grieve, bemoan
Mournful adj.	sad, sorrowful
Mouthpiece n.	speaker, spokesman
Move vb.	proceed, progress, push
Movement n.	move, motion
Mucilaginous adj.	slimy
Muffle vb.	deaden, soften, envelop
Multifarious adj.	multiform, manifold, various, diversified
Multiply vb.	increase, double, triple, trouble,
Multitude n.	crowd, mass, horde, mob, swarm
Munificent adj.	generous, bountiful, liberal

Murder n.	homicide, assassination, slaughter **vb.** kill, assassinate, slaughter
Murmur n.	mutter, mumble **vb.** mutter, mumble, grumble, whimper
Muse vb.	meditate, ponder
Mutable adj.	changeable, alterable, inconstant
Mutinous adj.	rebellious, revolutionary, unruly
Mutiny n.	rebellion, revolt, uprising **vb.** rebel, revolt, rise up
Mutual adj.	reciprocal, alternate
Myopic adj.	near-sighted, short-sighted
Mysterious adj.	secret, puzzling, strange
Myth n.	legend, tradition, fable, fiction

N

Nab vb.	catch, grasp
Nag vb.	annoy, pester, irritate, vex **n.** pest, nuisance
Naïve adj.	natural, simple, innocent
Naked adj.	undressed, bare, uncovered, nude, plain, unadorned
Name n. vb.	title, term, christen, designate
Nap n.	snooze, doze, siesta
Narcissistic adj.	egocentric, self-centered
Narrate vb.	tell, relate
Narrative n.	story, tale, account
Narrow adj.	slender, thin, taper

Narrow-minded adj.	close, close-minded, prejudiced, biased
Nation n.	country, state, realm, kingdom, republic, people, race, stock, society
Native adj.	natural, inborn, inbred, hereditary **n.** inhabitant, resident
Natural adj.	inherited, hereditary, basic, fundamental
Naturally adv.	normally, usually
Nature n.	world, universe, quality, essence, sort, manner, disposition
Nausea n.	queasiness, inclination to vomit
Navigate vb.	guide, steer, pilot
Near adj.	close, nearby, neighbouring, adjoining
Nearly adv.	almost, practically
Neat adj.	clean, orderly, tidy, orderly, well organised
Necessary adj.	needed, important, essential
Necessity n.	requirement, essential, prerequisite
Need n.	want, lack, necessity
Needle vb.	prod, provoke, goad, nag
Needless adj.	unnecessary, nonessential, superfluous
Needy adj.	poverty, stricken, destitute
Nefarious adj.	atrocious, wicked, villainous, dreadful, vile
Neglect vb.	ignore, omit, skip
Negotiate vb.	arrange, settle, transact, bargain

Nerve n.	impudence, rudeness, impertinence
Nervous adj.	timid, shy, fearful
Nestle vb.	snuggle, cuddle, snug
Neurotic adj.	psychoneurotic, disturb
Neutral adj.	uninvolved, nonpartisan
Neutralize vb.	counterbalance
New adj.	novel, fresh, unique
New-fangled adj.	new-made, new-fashioned
News n.	information, edge, date, report
Nice adj.	pleasant, agreeable
Nicety n.	exactness, truth, niceness
Nickname n.	sobriquet
Niggardly adj.	stingy, avaricious, penurious, close-fisted
Nihilism n.	nothingness, nothing, non-existence, nonentity
Nil n.	nothing, nought, zero, none
Nimble adj.	agile, spry, lively, quick
Nitwit n.	fool, idiot, simpleton
Noise n.	tumult, uproar, clamor, din, clatter, outcry
Noisy adj.	loud, clamorous, tumultuous
Nomad n.	wanderer, rover, gypsy
Nominate vb.	name, select
Nonbeliever n.	atheist, skeptic
Nondescript adj.	indescribable, indefinite, unclassifiable

Nonsense n.	trash, rubbish
Nonsensical adj.	ridiculous, absurd, silly, stupid, senseless
Nonstop adj.	endless, unceasing, continuous
Normal adj.	healthy, sound
Normally adv.	usually, customarily, regularly
Nosy adj.	prying, curious, inquisitive
Notable adj.	noteworthy, remark
Noted adj.	well-known, distinguished, famed
Notify vb.	inform, advise
Notion n.	idea, belief, view
Nourish vb.	sustain, support
Nourishment n.	sustenance, food, nutriment
Numerous adj.	many, infinite
Nurse vb.	take care of, tend, care for, attend
Nurture vb.	nourish, bring up, train up **n.** nursing, nourishing, tender, attention

O

Oath n.	pledge, promise, curse, profanity, swearword, expletive
Obdurate vb.	chide
Obedience n.	submission, docility
Obedient adj.	docile, yielding, respectful, obliging
Obese adj.	fat, overweight, plump
Object vb.	protest, disapprove of, complain **n.** goal, target, aim, thing

Objection n.	protest, disapproval
Objectionable adj.	offensive, improper, unbecoming
Objective n.	aim, goal, purpose **adj.** fair, just, impartial
Obligation n.	requirement, duty, contract
Oblige vb.	require, force, compel
Obliterate vb.	efface, erase, cancel, rub out, wipe out, strike out, wear out
Obscure adj.	unknown, inconspicuous, indistinct, dark, dim **vb.** dark, dim
Obsequious adj.	flattering, ingratiating
Observation n.	watching, attention
Observe vb.	see, notice, look at
Obstacle n.	block, stop, barrier, obstruction
Obstinate adj.	stubborn, inflexible
Obstruct vb.	block, stop, hinder, prevent, interfere
Obstruction n.	obstacle, block, blockage, barrier
Obtain vb.	acquire, gain, procure, secure, attain
Obviate vb.	forestall, prevent, obstruct
Obvious adv.	clearly, plainly, certainly
Occasion n.	time, occurrence
Occasional adj.	irregular, random, sporadic
Occasionally adj.	seldom, irregularly
Occupant n.	resident, tenant, inhabitant
Occupation n.	trade, profession, business, job, employment
Occupy vb.	take up, use, fill, hold, engage, busy, employ, absorb

Occur vb.	happen, take place
Occurrence n.	event, happening, incident
Odd adj.	strange, unusual, peculiar, queer, weird, extraordinary
Odds and ends n. phr.	fragments, remnants, scraps
Odour n.	smell, aroma, scent, fragrance, perfume
Off-colour adj.	risque, salty, earthy
Offend vb.	irritate, annoy, vex, anger, provoke
Offender n.	culprit, miscreant, criminal, lawbreaker
Offense n.	transgression, trepass, crime, wrongdoing, misdemeanor
Offer vb.	present, tender, proffer, submit **n.** suggestion, proposal, presentation
Officer n.	executive, manager, director, administrator
Officious adj.	meddlesome, interfering, obtrusive, meddling
Offset vb.	balance, counterbalance, set off
Offshoot n.	branch, by-product
Offspring n.	children, descendants, issue, progeny
Often adv.	frequently, oftentimes, regularly, usually
Old adj.	aged, elderly, dilapidated, ragged, faded, antique
Old-timer n.	veteran, master

Omen n.	suspice, sign, prognostic, augury, foreboding, portent
Omit vb.	leave out
Omniscient adj.	all-knowing
Onerous adj.	burdensome, oppressive, heavy
One-sided adj.	partial, prejudiced
Onlooker n.	observer, witness, bystander, spectator
Only adj.	sole, single, lone, solitary
Onset n.	beginning, start
Onus n.	burden, load, weight
Onward adv.	forward, ahead
Ooze vb.	seep, exude, drip
Open adj.	assessable, public, unfilled
Open-hearted adj.	frank, candid, honest
Open-minded adj.	fair, tolerant
Operate vb.	run, work, use
Opinion n.	belief, view, viewpoint
Opinionated adj.	prejudiced, biased
Opponent n.	rival, competitor, contestant, antagonist
Opportune adj.	appropriate, proper
Opportunity n.	chance, time, occasion
Oppose vb.	resist, battle, combat
Opposite adj.	contrary, reverse
Opposition n.	enemy, contestant

Oppress vb.	suppress, crush, persecute, burden, depress
Oppression n.	tyranny, injustice
Oppressive adj.	difficult, hard, stifling
Optimist n.	hopefulness, confidence
Opulence n.	wealth, affluence
Opulent adj.	rich, wealthy, prosperous, affluent, well-to-do
Oral adj.	spoken, uttered, verbal, vocal, voiced
Oration n.	speech, address, sermon, lecture
Orbit n.	course, path, circuit vb. circle, revolve
Ordain vb.	decree, declare
Ordeal n.	trial, test, assay, examination, experiment, scrutiny
Order n.	command, direction, merchandise, shipment
Orderly adj.	neat, well-organised, well-behaved
Ordinarily adj.	usually, commonly, generally
Ordinary adj.	average, mediocre, everyday, undistinguished
Orifice n.	aperture, perforation, pore, vent
Origin n.	beginning, source, root, cradle, birthplace, rise, start
Original adj.	first, primary, beginning, unique, new, fresh
Originate vb.	arise, begin, start, invent, create, begin

Originator n.	inventor, creator, discoverer
Ornamental adj.	decorative, ornate
Ostentatious adj.	boastful, flaunting, pompous
Ostracize vb.	banish, exile
Outcome n.	result, end, consequence
Outdo vb.	surpass, excel, beat
Outfit n.	gear, clothing, equipment **vb.** equip, supply, provide
Outgrowth n.	development, result, effect, product
Outlandish adj.	strange, weird, odd, peculiar
Outlaw n.	criminal **vb.** prohibit, ban
Outlook n.	viewpoint, prospect, chance, opportunity
Output n.	production, productivity, yield
Outrage n.	affront, offense, insult **vb.** shock, injure, offend
Outrageous adj.	shocking, offensive, disgraceful, shameful, shameless, gross
Outset n.	beginning, start, commencement
Outside n.	exterior, surface, covering, limit, bound
Outsmart vb.	outwit, outmanoeuvre
Outspoken adj.	plain, plainspoken, frank, blunt, candid
Outstanding adj.	well-known, famous, prominent
Outwit vb.	confuse, trick, baffle
Overall adj.	general, complete, comprehensive
Overcast adj.	cloudy
Overcome vb.	conquer, defeat, beat, subdue
Overhaul vb.	revamp, rebuild

Overlook vb.	disregard, neglect
Overpower vb.	overwhelm, vanquish, overcome, conquer
Overrule vb.	reverse, revoke
Oversee vb.	supervise, manager, operate
Overseer n.	supervisor, manage, foreman, superintendent
Oversight n.	error, overlooking, omission, blunder, neglect, fault
Overtake vb.	catch, reach, pass
Overthrow vb.	overpower, defeat, conquer, upset, feat, collapse
Overture n.	offer, proposal
Overwhelm vb.	defeat, overcome, overpower, bury
Own vb.	possess, have hold

P

Peace n.	rate, velocity
Pacific adj.	peaceful, calm, tranquil, quit
Pacify vb.	calm, quiet, tranquilize, smooth, lull
Pack vb.	stow, stuff, compress **n.** bundle, package, parcel
Package n.	bundle, parcel
Packet n.	package, bundle
Pact n.	agreement, contract, compact, arrangement, treaty, bargain
Pad n.	cushion, wadding, stuffing, filling, padding

Paddle n.	sweep, oar
Pageant n.	spectacle, exhibition, show, display, extravaganza
Painful adj.	agonizing, aching, inflamed, sore, throbbing
Painstaking adj.	careful, exacting, scrupulous
Palatial adj.	luxurious, majestic
Pale adj.	white, ashen, colourless, wan
Pallid adj.	wan, pale, whitish, colorless
Palpitate vb.	pulsate, throb, flutter, beat, tremble, quiver, shiver
Paltry adj.	meager, petty, trivial, trifling, insignificant
Pamper vb.	baby, coddle, spoil
Pamphlet n.	brochure, booklet, leaflet
Panacea n.	cure-all, universal, remedy
Pang n.	pain, hurt, throb
Panic n.	alarm, fear, dread, fright, terror **vb.** terrify, frighten, alarm
Panorama n.	complete view
Pant vb.	puff, gasp, wheeze
Pantry n.	storeroom, cupboard, scullery
Paradigm n.	example, pattern
Paradise n.	heaven, utopia
Paralyze vb.	deaden, numb, freeze
Parcel n.	package, bundle, packet
Pare vb.	peel, skin, diminish, reduce, cut, trim, crop
Parity n.	equality, equivalence, likeness, sameness, analogy

Parley vb.	talk, converse, discourage, discuss, confer
Parsimony n.	stinginess, avarice, covetousness, meanness, frugality, miserliness
Part n.	portion, piece, section, fraction, fragment **vb.** divide, split, breakup
Partake vb.	participate, share, have a share of, participate in
Participant n.	shareholder, partner, associate, colleague
Participate vb.	share, partake, join, engage in
Particle n.	bit, spot, grain, speak, shred, scrap
Particular adj.	special, distinct, careful, especial, special **n.** detail, point, item, feature
Particularly adv.	especially, specially
Partisan n.	follower, disciple, supporter, backer **adj.** partial
Partition n.	division, separation, distribution
Partly adv.	partially, somewhat, comparatively
Partner n.	associate, colleague, participant
Part with vb. phr.	relinquish, resign, surrender, give up
Party n.	group, gathering, crowd, block, organization
Passé adj.	old-fashioned, old hat, out-of-date
Passion n.	emotion, feeling, rapture, excitement, love
Passionate adj.	emotional, excited, impulsive, zealous, earnest, sincere

Pass muster vb. phr.	answer, do well enough
Password n.	watch, counter sign, secret, parole
Past adj.	gone, over, finished
Pastime n.	amusement, recreation, entertainment, hobby
Patch n. vb.	mend, repair
Patent n.	protection, copyright, permit **vb.** license, limit, copyright
Path n.	walk, trail, track, pathway, walkway
Pathetic adj.	pitiful, touching
Pathos n.	passion, warmth of feeling, tender, emotion
Patience n.	composure, serenity, passiveness, endurance, perseverance, persistence
Patrol vb.	guard, watch, inspect
Patron n.	customer, client, backer
Patronize vb.	buy at, support
Paucity n.	fewness, rarity, poverty, insufficiency, smallness of quantity
Pause n.	hesitation, interruption **vb.** hesitate, rest
Pawn n.	tool, cat's paw
Pay vb.	settle, remit, discharge, reward, compensate, recompense, return **n.** payment, salary, wage, wages
Payable adj.	due, owed
Peace n.	quiet, serenity, calm, peacefulness, tranquility

Peaceable adj.	peaceful, gentle, mild, truce
Peaceful adj.	peaceable, quiet, calm, serene, tranquil
Peace-offering n.	atonement, amends, respiration
Peak n.	top, summit, point, crest
Peculiar adj.	unusual, odd, strange, unfamiliar, uncommon, queer, outlandish
Peculiarity n.	characteristic, distinctiveness
Pedagogue n.	schoolmaster, teacher, instructor, pedant
Pedigree n.	family, descent, ancestry, parentage, line, lineage
Peek n. vb.	peel, peer, glimpse
Peel n.	skin, rind, peeling
Peep vb. n.	chirp, squeak
Peer n.	equal, parallel, match
Peeve vb.	irritate, annoy, vex, irk
Pen n.	enclosure, cage, coop, sty
Penalize vb.	punish, dock
Penalty n.	punishment, forfeit, fine
Penetrate vb.	enter, bore, permeate, spread
Penetrating adj.	piercing, boring, puncturing, sharp
Peninsula n.	point, neck, spit
Penniless adj.	poor, poverty, stricken, needy, destitute
Penury n.	indigence, destitution, extreme, poverty, want
People n.	human beings, persons, beings, race, nation, tribe, clan, family

Perception n.	understanding, comprehension, discernment
Perceptive adj.	discerning, observant
Percolate vb.	filter, ooze, exude, perpetrate, strain, drain, penetrate
Perdition n.	ruin, destruction, overthrow, wreck, demolition, downfall
Peregrination n.	travelling, wandering, journey, roaming, tour
Perfectionist n.	purist, pedant, precisionist
Perforate vb.	pierce, penetrate, drill, punch, puncture
Performance n.	presentation, offering, exhibition, appearance
Performer n.	actor/actress, entertainer
Perfunctory adj.	formal, mechanical, superficial
Perhaps adv.	maybe, possibly, conceivably
Peril n.	danger, hazard, risk
Perilous adj.	dangerous, risky, hazardous, unsafe
Period n.	time, interval, era, age, epoch, course, cycle, timing
Periphery n.	outside, outer, boundary, circumference
Perish vb.	die, expire, pass away, depart
Perishable adj.	decayable, decomposable
Permanent adj.	enduring, stable, continuing, everlasting, unchanging, unaltered, invariable

Permission n.	consent, leave
Permissive adj.	lenient, tolerant, easy, unrestrictive
Permit vb.	allow, let, tolerate
Perpendicular adj.	vertical, upright, standing
Perpetual adj.	unceasing, continuing, permanent, constant, ceaseless, undying
Perplex vb.	confuse, puzzle, mystify, bewilder
Persecute vb.	oppress, torment
Persevere vb.	endure, persist,
Persiflage n. fr.	Banter, ridicule, jeering, mockery
Persist vb.	preserve, continue, endure
Persistent adj.	persevering, persisting
Person n.	human, human being, individual, personage, someone, somebody
Persuade vb.	influence, induce, convince, urge, coax, prompt
Persuasive adj.	convincing, influential, winning, alluring
Pert adj.	brisk, smart, impudent, flippant
Perturbed adj.	upset, flustered, disturbed, agitated
Pest n.	nuisance, irritate, annoyance, tease, bother
Pester vb.	annoy, irritate, vex, harass, trouble
Petrify vb.	paralyze, change to stone, stun
Peety adj.	unimportant, trivial, insignificant, paltry, trifling

Phlegmatic adj.	lethargic, listless, sluggish, slow, lazy
Phony adj.	fake, counterfeit, bogus
Physical adj.	bodily, corporeal, corporal
Picture n.	painting, drawing, illustration
Piece n.	quantity, unit, section, portion, part
Piecemeal adv.	partially, gradually
Pierce vb.	perforate, puncture, affect, rouse
Pigheaded adj.	stubborn, obstinate, inflexible
Pile n.	heap, collection, accumulation **vb.** heap
Pilgrim n.	traveller, wanderer
Pilgrimage n.	tour, journey, trip, expedition
Pillar n.	column, shaft, support, prop
Pillow n.	cushion, bolster
Pin n.	fastening, fastener, clip, peg, brooch, tiepin, stickpin
Pinnacle n.	top, summit, apex, zenith, highest, point
Pioneer n.	pathfinder, explorer
Piquant n.	biting, piercing, sharp, cutting, pungent, sharp, stimulating
Pique n.	resentment, grudge, stinging vexation **vb.** irritate, vex
Pit n.	hole, cavity, hollow, well, excavation
Pit against vb. phr.	set to fight, set in opposition, match for a contest
Pitch vb.	setup, establish

Pitcher n.	jug
Pitiful adj.	pitiable, pathetic, distressing
Pitiless adj.	merciless, unmerciful, ruthless, mean, cruel, hard-hearted
Pity n.	sympathy, compassion, mercy, tenderhearted
Pivotal adj.	central, focal, crucial, critical, essential
Place n.	space, plot, region **vb.** put, set, arrange, locate
Placid adj.	quiet, tranquil, unreffled
Plaint n.	lamentation, lament, moan, wail
Plan n.	plot, procedure, scheme, design, method **vb.** scheme, design
Plane n.	level, airplane
Platform n.	dais, stage, pulpit
Playful adj.	frolicsome, sportive
Plaything n.	game, gadget
Plea n.	appeal, request, pleading
Plead vb.	beg, entreat, appeal
Pleasant adj.	enjoyable, nice, agreeable, pleasurable, amiable, friendly
Please vb.	gratify, satisfy, wish
Pleasing adj.	pleasant, agreeable
Pleasure n.	delight, satisfaction, gratification, luxury, indulgence
Pledge n.	promise, agreement, oath **vb.** promise, swear, vow

Plentiful adj.	abundant, bountiful, fullness
Plenty n.	abundance, fullness, fruitfulness, bounty, plentifulness
Plight n.	predicament, dilemma, situation, state, condition
Plod vb.	trudge, persist, persevere
Pluck vb.	snatch, pull, jerk **n.** bravery, nerve, determination, spirit
Plucky adj. colloq.	Brave, spirited, courageous
Plug n.	stopper **vb.** stop, obstruct
Plumb adj.	chubby, fat, stout, portly, fleshy
Plunder vb.	rob, pillage, sack, raid, loot **n.** spoils, pillage
Plunge vb.	immerse, dive, jump
Pocketbook n.	handbag, purse, wallet
Poem n.	verse, poetry, lyric
Poetry n.	verse, meter
Point n.	locality, position, location, aim, object **vb.** indicate, show, designate, direct, guide, head, lead
Point-break adv.	directly, bluntly, explicitly, plainly
Pointless adj.	purposeless, vain
Poise n.	self-control, control, composure, dignity **vb.** balance, hesitate
Poke n. vb.	stab, thrust, punch
Policy n.	tactic, strategy, procedure

Polish vb.	shine, brighten, refine, finish **n.** gloss, shine, sheen, luster, elegance
Polite adj.	courteous, thoughtful, mannerly, considerate, cordial
Ponder vb.	weigh, consider
Ponderous adj.	heavy, weighty
Populous adj.	thronged, crowded, teeming, dense
Porch n.	veranda, patio
Portable adj.	movable, transportable, handy
Portend vb.	foretoken, foreshadow
Portentous adj.	momentous, significant, critical
Portion n.	share, part, allotment, quota, section, segment, serving **vb.** allot, deal out
Portly adj.	dignified, grand, corpulent, fat, heavy, obese
Portrait n.	picture, likeness, representation
Portray vb.	represent, depict
Pose vb.	pretend, act, assert **n.** posture, position
Poser n.	enigma, mystery
Positively adv.	absolutely, certainly, surely
Possess vb.	have, own, occupy, control
Possessed adj.	haunted, enchanted, entranced, obsessed
Possession n.	ownership, occupancy, custody, property
Possible adj.	practical, practicable, feasible

Possibly adv.	may be, perhaps, perchance
Posterity n.	descendants, progeny, succeeding
Postpone vb.	delay, defer
Pot n.	saucepan, kettle
Potent adj.	powerful, strong, mighty, influential
Potential adj.	hidden, dormant
Pouch n.	sack, bag, container
Pound vb.	beat, strike, , hit
Pour vb.	flow
Pout vb.	sulk, brood, mope
Poverty n.	destitution, scarcity, scarceness
Power n.	ability, capability, force, strength, might, vigour, rule, sovereignty
Powerful adj.	strong, mighty, influential, effective
Practical adj.	workable, achievable, attainable
Practically adv.	nearly, almost
Practice n.	habit, custom, usage
Practised adj.	skilled, adept, expert, able
Prairie n.	grassland, plain
Praise vb.	commend, loud, applaud, admire, celebrate **n.** evaluate, value, assay
Preach vb.	moralize, lecture, teach, urge
Preamble n.	introduction, prelude, prologue
Precaution n.	forethought, care, foresight
Precedence n.	priority, preference
Precedent n.	example, model
Precinct n.	confine, boundary, enclosure

Precious adj.	valuable, costly, priceless, expensive
Precipice n.	cliff, bluff, crag
Precipitate adj.	swift, hasty, speedy **vb.** hurry, acceleration, expedite
Precipitous adj.	steep, abrupt
Precise adj.	definite, exact
Precisely adv.	exactly, specifically
Precision n.	exactness, accuracy
Precursor n.	forerunner, predecessor, antecedent, harbinger, herald, pioneer, presage
Predatory adj.	plundering, pillaging
Predicament n.	dilemma, plight, condition
Predict vb.	foretell, prophesy, forecast
Prediction n.	prophecy, forecast
Predominant adj.	prevalent, dominant, prevailing
Predominate vb.	outweigh, prevail, rule
Prefer vb.	favour, select, elect
Preference n.	choice, selection
Prejudice n.	bias, partiality, unfairness
Preliminary adj.	preparatory, introductory
Premature adj.	untimely, early, unexpected
Preoccupied adj.	distracted, inattentive meditative
Prepare vb.	ready, arrange
Prerequisite n.	requirement, essential, necessity, demand
Prescribe vb.	direct, designate, order
Presence n.	attendance, nearness, appearance
Present adj.	existing, current

Present vb.	grant, display n. gift, donation, gratuity
Presentable adj.	polite, well-mannered, respectable
Presently adv.	soon, shortly, right away, directly, immediately
Preserve vb.	conserve, save
Preside vb.	direct, officiate, administrate
Press vb.	squeeze, urge, insist on n. pressure, urgency, journalist, the fourth estate, reporters, news reporters
Prestige b.	reputation, importance, distinction, renown
Presume vb.	suppose, assume
Presumption n.	supposition, assumption
Presumptuous adj.	bold, impudent
Pretend vb.	imagine, feign
Pretense n.	deceit, fabrication, lie, falsehood, deception
Pretentious adj.	ostentatious, show-off, gaudy
Pretty adj.	attractive, fair, lovely, beautiful
Prevail vb.	predominate, succeed, win
Prevailing adj.	general, regular
Prevalent adj.	common, prevailing, widespread, extensive
Prevaricate vb.	shuffle, equivocate, shift, deviate
Prevent vb.	block, stop, thwart, hinder, inhibit
Prey n.	victim
Prey on vb. phr.	victimize, seize, raid

Price n.	cost, charge, expense, value **vb.** value, rate
Pride n.	conceit, vanity, arrogance, self-importance, egotism
Prim adj.	strait-laced, formal
Primness n.	formality, affected
Prima facie *l.*	at first sight, on the first view
Primarily adv.	chiefly, mainly
Primary adj.	chief, main, principal, first, fundamental, beginning
Prime adj.	first, chief
Primitive adj.	primeval, uncivilised, uncultured, rough
Primordial adj.	first in order, element
Principal adj.	chief, main, leading, prime, first **n.** chief, head, leader, headmaster
Principle n.	rule, standard, law, law, axiom
Print vb.	issue, publish, reissue, reprint, letter **n.** fingerprint, sign, type
Prior adj.	earlier, sooner
Prison n.	jail
Private adj.	personal, special, confidential
Privilege n.	freedom, right, advantage
Privacy adj.	knowledge, cognizance
Prize n.	reward, award **vb.** value, esteem, rate, estimate
Probable adj.	likely, presumable
Probe vb.	investigate, inquire, scrutinize
Problem n.	difficulty, predicament, dilemma

Procedure n.	operation, conduct, management, method, system
Proceed vb.	move ahead
Proceedings n. pl.	record, annual, document
Proceeds n. pl.	income, procedure, method, system
Process n.	course, procedure, method, system **vb.** treat, prepare
Procession n.	parade, cavalcade
Proclaim vb.	announce, advertise, declare, publish
Proclamation n.	announcement, promulgation
Procrastinate vb.	vacillate, hesitate, waver, stall, defer
Prod vb.	nudge, goad, push
Producer vb.	bear, bring forth, yield, supply, give **n.** production, fruits
Productive adj.	fertile, fruitful, rich
Profanity n.	blasphemy
Profess vb.	declare, state, avow
Profession n.	occupation, vocation, employment
Profit n.	gain, return, earning, benefit, gain
Profitable adj.	gainful, benefit
Profound adj.	deep, solemn, serious, wise
Program n.	schedule, record, plan, calendar
Progress n.	advance, movement, improvement **vb.** proceed, develop
Prohibit vb.	forbid, disallow, hinder
Prohibition n.	ban, prevention, restriction, embargo

Prolific adj.	fruitful, fertile, productive
Prolong vb.	lengthen, extend, increase
Promise n.	assurance, pledge, oath, vow, word **vb.** pledge, vow, assure, swear
Promote vb.	advance, further, support, help, aid, assist, raise, elevate, advance
Promulgate vb.	publish, announce, proclaim, declare, advertise
Prone adj.	incline, apt, like, disposed, predisposed
Pronounce vb.	utter, proclaim, announce, articulate, utter, enunciate
Pronounced adj.	definite, clear, noticeable
Proper adj.	suitable, correct, fitting, just, polite, decent, well-mannered
Prophecy n.	prediction, augury
Prophesy vb.	predict, foretell, divine, augur
Prophet n.	oracle, fortuneteller, forecaster, seer, clairvoyant, soothsayer
Propitious adj.	advantageous, opportune, favourable, promising
Proposal n.	offer, suggestion, programme, scheme, plan
Propose vb.	present, offer, tender, recommend, suggest, plan, intend, expect, mean
Proprietor n.	owner, manager, businesswoman/man
Prosaic adj.	common, commonplace, ordinary, everyday, outline
Proscribe vb.	ban, forbid, disallow, prohibit

Prospect n.	expectation, anticipation, buyer, candidate **vb.** search, explore, dig
Prospective adj.	proposed, planned, hoped for
Prosper vb.	succeed, thrive, rise, flourish
Prosperous adj.	wealthy, well-off, rich, thriving, flourishing, well-to-do
Prostrate adj.	supine, prone, recumbent, overcome, overwhelmed, crushed
Protect vb.	shield, guard, defend
Protection n.	guard, security, shield, safety, assurance, safeguard
Protuberance n.	projection, prominence, bulge, swelling, protrusion
Prove vb.	show, demonstrate, confirm, verify, affirm, test, examine, try
Proverb n.	saying, adage, maxim, byword
Proverbial adj.	well-known, common, general
Provide vb.	supply, furnish, equip, give, bestow
Provision n.	arrangement, condition
Provisions n. pl.	store, supplies, stock
Proviso n.	condition, provision, clause, conditional stipulation
Provoke vb.	bother, vex, irritate, annoy, irk, anger, enrage, cause, occasion, bring about
Prowess n.	bravery, valour, courage, gallantry, daring
Prowl vb.	slink, sneak, lurk
Proximity n.	nearness, vicinity, neighbourhood
Proxy n.	substitute, agent, deputy, delegate, representative, attorney

Prudent adj.	wise, discreet, careful, sensible, provident, reasonable
Prudish n.	formal, prim, straitlaced
Pry vb.	peep, peer, peek, meddle
Publish vb.	issue, distribute, bring out, announce, declare, proclaim, disclose, reveal, publicize
Pucker vb.	corrugate, furrow, cockle, wrinkle, gather into wrinkles or folds, gather
Pugilism n.	boxing, fighting with the fist, prize-fighting
Pull vb.	drag, draw **n.** (informal) influence, weight, wrench, jerk, haul, tow
Pull apart vb. phr.	separate, divide
Pull away vb. phr.	leave, depart
Pull down vb. phr.	wreck, destroy, raze
Pull off n. phr.	remove
Pull out n. phr.	leave, depart
Pull through vb. phr.	survive, recover
Pull up vb. phr.	stop
Pull in one's horns, colloq.	repress one's ardor, restrain one's pride, cease boasting
Punctual adj.	prompt, timely, on time
Pupil n.	student, learner, undergraduate
Purchase vb.	buy, obtain, get, acquire, procure **n.** buying, shopping, acquisition

Purely adv.	completely, entirely, totally
Puritanical adj.	strait-laced, stiff, prim
Purpose n.	intension, intent, object, end, aim, objective, goal, use, application
On purpose n. phr.	intention, ally, deliberately
Pursue vb.	follow, chase, hound, track
Pursuit n.	chase, hunt
Push vb.	force, shove, thrust, press, hove
Put vb.	place, set, attach, establish, assign, express, state, say
Put aside vb. phr.	save, keep
Put down vb. phr.	defeat, repress
Put off vb. phr.	delay, postpone, discount
Put on vb. phr.	don, dress, attire, pretend, fake, feign, stage, produce, present
Put out vb. phr.	extinguish, douse, discomfort, inconvenience, extend, offer, eject, discard
Put up vb. phr.	preserve, can, smoke, pickle, erect, build, construct
Put up with vb. phr.	endure, stand, tolerate, suffer
Putrid adj.	rotten, decayed, decomposed, moldy, putrefied, stinking
Puzzling adj.	baffling, enigmatic, perplexing
Pygmean adj.	dwarfish, dwarfed, diminutive, small, stunted, pygmy, little

Q

Quack n.	fake, faker, fraud, impostor, charlatan
Quail vb.	cower, shrink, flinch, faint, drop, quake, tremble, give way, lose courage, lose spirit
Quaint adj.	strange, unusual, odd, curious, uncommon, antiquated, antique, picturesque, old-fashioned
Quake vb.	tremble, shake, quiver, shudder **n.** earthquake, temblor
Qualified adj.	capable, efficient, competent, fit, suited, suitable
Qualify vb.	suit, fit, befit, limit, restrict, change
Quantity n.	amount, extent, mass, bulk, measure, number
Queasy adj.	nauseated, qualmish, inclined to vomit, sick, fastidious, squeamish, delicate, sensitive
Queer adj.	odd, peculiar, unusual, uncommon, extraordinary
Quench vb.	satisfy, slake, allay, slake, cool, extinguish, damper
Query n.	inquiry, question **vb.** inquire, question, ask
Quest n.	search, journey, hunt
Quick adj.	rapid, swift, fast, speedy, impatient, abrupt, hasty, curt, prompt, ready, immediate

Quick-witted adj.	shrewd, astute, clever, acute
Quintessence n.	essence, essential, part, extract
Quip n.	taunt, gibe, jeer, sneer, scoff, mock, retort, sarcasm, witticism
Quirk n.	evasion, subterfuge, shift, prevarication, quibble, loophole, pretence, pretext, excuse, taunt, gibe, jeer, quip
Quit vb.	leave, depart, vacate, stop, cease, discontinue, resign, leave
Quite adv.	rather, somewhat, completely, entirely, wholly
Quota n.	portion, share, allotment, apportionment, quantity

R

Race n.	contest, competition, meet, match **vb.** run, complete, speed, dash, hasten
Race n.	family, breed, people, nation, tribe, stock
Racist adj.	bigoted, prejudiced, fanatic
Rack n.	framework, frame, bracket
Racketeer n.	gangster
Radiant adj.	bright, shining, beaming, brilliant
Radiate vb.	emit, spread, shed
Rag n.	remnant, cloth
Rage n.	anger, fury, wrath **vb.** fume, rant, rave, storm

Ragged adj.	tattered, shredded, worn
Raid n.	attack, assault, invasion **vb.** attack, assault
Rail n.	fence, railing
Rail at vb. phr.	censure, reproach, sneer at
Rain n.	drizzle, shower
Raise vb.	lift, elevate, hoist **n.** increase, rise
Rakish adj.	dashing, dapper, debonair, smart
Ramble vb.	saunter, wander, walk **n.** stroll, walk
Rambling adj.	incoherent, disjointed, erratic
Ramify vb.	branch, devaricate
Rancor n.	malignity, malice, spite, enmity, animosity, vindictiveness, bitterness
Random adj.	chance, haphazard
Range n.	extent, expanse, area **vb.** change, wander
Rank n.	grade, level, order **adj.** wild, dense, lush, offensive, foul, rotten
Ransom n.	deliverance, release, compensation **vb.** redeem
Rant vb.	rave, fume, harangue
Rap n.	knock, blow, thump **vb.** knock, cuff, thump, whack
Rapture n.	joy, bliss, ecstasy, delight
Rare adj.	unusual, uncommon, scarce, infrequent, matchless
Rascal n.	villain, scoundrel, rouge, trickster, swindler
Rash adj.	thoughtless, hasty, reckless

Rash n.	eruption, eczema, dermatitis
Rate n.	pace, speed, velocity **vb.** price, value, rank, evaluate
Ration n.	allowance, portion
Rational adj.	sensible, reasonable, normal
Rave vb.	rant, rage, storm, praise
Ravel vb.	disentangle, untwist, unravel, unweave
Ravine n.	gorge, chasm, canyon
Ravishing adj.	captivating, enchanting, bewitching
Ray n.	beam
Raze vb.	demolish, destroy
Reach vb.	arrive at, get to, stretch, extend
React vb.	respond, reply
Reaction n.	response, result, reception
Ready adj.	prepared, done, completed, quick **vb.** prepare, arrange
Real adj.	true, actual, genuine, authentic
Realise vb.	actualize, perfect, appreciate, recognize
Really adv.	actually, truly, honestly
Realm n.	kingdom, domain, domain, sphere, province
Reap vb.	harvest, cut, gather
Rear vb.	raise, bring up, lift, elevate, rise, build
Reasonable adj.	sensible, rational, moderate, bearable
Rebel n.	revolutionary, mutineer

Rebuff n.	repulse, check, snub, refusal, rejection repulse **vb.** repel, resist, reject
Rebut vb.	repel, rebuff, repel, retort, oppose, disprove
Recalcitrant adj.	opposing, refractory, disobedient
Recall vb.	remember, recollect, **n.** recollection, remembrance
Recapitulate vb.	repeat, reiterate, rehearse, restate, sum up
Recede vb.	retreat, retire
Receive vb.	accept, get, acquire, obtain, entertain
Recent adj.	late, up-to-date
Receptacle n.	repository, depository, receiver, vessel, container
Reception n.	party, gathering
Recess n.	hollow, niche, dent **vb.** hollow, indent
Recess n.	respite, rest, period, pause, break
Recession n.	depression, downturn, slowdown
Recipe n.	formula, instruction
Reciprocal adj.	mutual, complementary, correlative, interchangeable, alternate
Reckless adj.	thoughtless, careless, rash, wild
Reckoning n.	counting, computation, calculation, arrangement, settlement
Recluse n.	hermit, anchorite, loner
Recognize vb.	recollect, recall
Recoil from vb. phr.	abhor, loathe, abominate, detest, shrink from, hate

Recollect vb.	remember
Reconcile vb.	unite, bring together, mediate, adjust, adapt, settle
Recondition vb.	overhaul, rebuild, service, restore
Record vb.	enter, register **n.** recording, document
Recoup vb.	recover, regain, retrieve, repay
Recover vb.	regain, retrieve, redeem
Recreation n.	amusement, entertainment, diversion
Recruit n.	beginner, trainee
Rectitude n.	right, uprightness, integrity, honesty, equity, straightforwardness
Recumbent adj.	reclining, prostrate, listless, idle
Recuperate vb.	recover, rally, convalesce, improve
Reduce vb.	lessen, diminish, lower, degrade, downgrade
Reek vb.	smell, stink
Refer vb.	direct, commend, relate
Referee n.	umpire, arbitrator, arbiter, judge **vb.** umpire, judge
Reference n.	direction, allusion, mention
Refine vb.	improve, clarify, purify
Refined adj.	cultivated, polite, courteous, well-bred
Reflect vb.	mirror, ponder, cogitate
Refrain vb.	cease
Refresh vb.	renew, exhilarate, invigorate
Refreshment n.	snack, food, drink
Refuge n.	safety, shelter

Refund vb.	repay, reimburse, pay, restore, return, repay, give back
Refuse vb.	turn down, deny, disallow, decline
Refuse n.	garbage, waste, rubbish, trash
Refute vb.	confute, disprove, rebut, overthrow
Regal adj.	majestic, royal
Regard vb.	consider, estimate, attend **n.** reference, relation, concern, esteem
Regardless adj.	despite, notwithstanding
Regenerate vb.	reproduce, revive, change **adj.** reproduced, converted, regenerated
Regimen n.	dietetics, regulation, diet, fare, hygiene
Regimented adj.	orderly, ordered, rigid, controlled, disciplined
Region n.	area, place, locate, territory
Register n.	record, catalog, list, book, record, roll
Regret vb.	lament, bemoan **n.** sorrow, remorse, concern
Regrettable adj.	unfortunate, lamentable, deplorable
Regular adj.	usual, customary, normal, habitual
Regulate vb.	govern, control, manage, legislate
Regulation n.	law, rule, statute, direction, rule, order
Regurgitate vb.	flow back, be poured back
Rehearse vb.	practice, repeat, train
Reign n.	rule, dominion, sovereignty, power
Reject vb.	refuse, deny, renounce, discard, expel

Rejoice vb.	delight, enjoy
Relate vb.	tell, report, narrate
Relative adj.	proportional, dependent, in regard to
Relax vb.	loosen, slacken
Relaxation n.	ease, comfort
Relent vb.	yield, give, bend, relax
Reliable adj.	trustworthy, dependable
Reliance n.	dependence, trust, confidence, assurance, credence
Relief n.	ease, comfort
Religion n.	faith, belief
Relinquish vb.	leave, quit, vacate, desert, abandon, renounce, forbear, give up
Relish n.	satisfaction, delight, appreciation
Reluctant adj.	unwilling, disinclined
Remain vb.	stay, continue, linger
Reminder n.	residue, leftover, rest
Remand vb.	send back, consign
Remark vb.	say, mention, state, note, observe **n.** comment, statement, observation
Remarkable adj.	unusual, special, extraordinary, noteworthy, uncommon
Remedy n.	cure, medicine, relief, medication **vb.** cure, correct
Remember vb.	recall, recollect, memorize
Remembrance n.	recollection, recall, memory, momento
Remit vb.	pay, send forward
Remittance n.	payment

Remnant n.	reminder, residue, rest
Remodel vb.	renovate, redecorate, change, modify
Remonstrate vb.	protest
Remote adj.	distant, far off or away
Removed adj.	distant, aloof
Remuneration n.	payment, wages, salary, pay, compensation
Render vb.	perform, supply, deliver
Rendition n.	version, interpretation
Renegade n.	apostate, deserter, revolter, traitor
Renounce vb.	give up, abandon, abdicate, forsake, forgo
Renown n.	fame, repute, reputation, glory, distinction, prestige
Rent n.	rental, payment
Repair vb.	mend, patch, restore, renew, adjust
Repartee n.	banter
Repeal vb.	cancel, abolish **n.** cancellation, abolition
Replenish vb.	refill, renew, resupply, supply
Replica n.	copy, duplicate, reproduction, facsimile
Reporter n.	journalist, news (wo) man, newspaper (wo) man
Repose n.	sleep, rest, slumber
Reprehend vb.	reprove, rebuke, reproach, upbraid, reprimand
Reprieve vb.	respite, delay, relieve **n.** respite, suspension

Representative n.	agent, delegate, surrogate
Repudiate vb.	discard, reject, disclaim, renounce
Repulsive adj.	repellent, offensive, horrid
Reputable adj.	honest, straightforward, trustworthy, reliable
Require vb.	need, want, demand, order, call for, demand, need
Requirement n.	need, demand, necessity, condition, prerequisite, provision
Rescue vb.	save, set free, liberate, release, ransom, deliver **n.** liberation, release, ransom, deliverance, recovery
Resemblance n.	similarity, likeness
Resemble vb.	take after, look like
Resentment n.	bitterness, displeasure, indignation
Reserve vb.	save, keep, hold, maintain
Reserved adj.	restrained, straitlaced, proper
Reside vb.	abide, dwell, live, stay, lie, abide
Residence n.	home, abode, dwelling, stay, sojourn
Residue n.	remainder, balance, rest
Resign vb.	quit, abdicate, leave, abandon
Resigned adj.	forbearing, accepting, tolerant, reconciled
Resilient adj.	rebounding, recoiling, elastic, buoyant, springy
Resolute adj.	resolved, firm, determined, set, decided
Resource n.	preserve, store, supply, source
Resourceful adj.	ingenious, inventive, creative

Respectable adj.	acceptable, proper, decent, respected, fair, passable, presentable
Respectful adj.	polite, courteous, well bred, well-behaved, well-mannered
Respond vb.	reply, answer, acknowledge
Response n.	reply, answer, acknowledgement
Rest n.	remainder, residue, surplus, excess
Restful adj.	quiet, peaceful, calm, tranquil
Restrain vb.	control, check, churb, hold
Restraint n.	control, self-control, reserve, constraint
Restrict vb.	limit, confine, restrain
Result n.	effect, outcome, consequence **vb.** arise, happen, follow, issue
Resume vb.	continue, restart, reassume, recommence
Resuscitate vb.	revive, restore, resurrect
Retain vb.	hold, keep, remember, recall, hire, employ, engage
Retaliate vb.	revenge, reply, return, avenge
Retard vb.	delay, hold back, slow, hinder, check, obstruct
Retarded adj.	backward, slow behindhand, slow-witted, dull, stupid
Reticent adj.	reserved, quiet, silent, close-mouth, taciturn
Retire vb.	leave, part, withdraw, retreat, resign, leave
Retired adj.	withdraw, removed, abstracted, superannuated

Retiring adj.	shy, withdrawn, modest, reserved
Retrieve vb.	recover, regain, recapture
Revel in vb.	delight in, rejoice in, enjoy
Revelry n.	carousal, carouse, revel, festivity, orgy, noisy festivity
Revenue n.	income, take, profit, receipt, proceeds, return
Revere vb.	venerate, respect, admire
Reverence n.	respect, homage, veneration
Reverent adj.	respectful, honouring
Revive vb.	renew, refresh, reanimate, rejuvenate, reawaken, recover, rewake
Revolve vb.	turn, rotate, spin, cycle, circle
Revolver n.	pistol, six-shooter, six-gun, gun
Reward n.	prize, award, recompense, pay **vb.** compensate, pay
Rhyme n.	verse, poem, poetry, similarity in sound
Rich adj.	wealthy, affluent, abundant, plentiful
Rickety adj.	unsteady, unsound, unstable, flimsy
Riot n.	disorder, disturbance, tumult, uproar
Riotous adj.	tumultuous, turbulent, rebellious, disorderly
Rip vb. n.	cut, tear, slit, slash
Ripe adj.	ready, mature
Ripen vb.	mature, age, mellow
Ripple vb.	ruffle, wave
Risible adj.	laughable, ridiculous, ludicrous, comical, funny

Risk n.	peril, danger, hazard
Rival n.	contestant, antagonist, opponent
Rivalry n.	competition, contention, contest
Roar vb.	below, cry, shout
Rob vb.	steal, pilfer, rifle, sack
Robbery n.	theft, pillage, plundering, burglary
Robust adj.	strong, athletic, vigorous, energetic, powerful
Rod n.	pole, bar, wand, staff
Rogue n.	rascal, criminal, scoundrel
Room n.	chamber, enclosure, space
Root n.	cause, origin, basis, reason
Rooted adj.	steadfast, fixed, firm, stationary, immovable
Rosy adj.	pink, reddish, fresh, ruddy, cheerful
Rot vb.	spoil, decompose, decay
Rotate vb.	turn, revolve, spin
Rotten adj.	moldy, decayed, tainted, corrupt, immoral
Rotund adj.	round, spherical, plumb, full, obese, stout
Rough adj.	uneven, unpolished, crude, unrefined, stormy, turbulent
Roughly adv.	about, approximately, nearly
Roundabout adj.	indirect
Rouse vb.	awaken, waken
Routine n.	way, method, system, habit
Rover n.	wander, rank, file, order

Row n.	quarrel, spat, disturbance
Rubbish n.	waste, garbage, litter, debris, trash
Rubicund adj.	ruddy, reddish, florid
Ruffian n.	brawling, rowdy, disorderly
Rug n.	carpet, floor-covering
Rugged adj.	rough, harsh, tough
Rule n.	ruling, law, regular
Ruler n.	leader, governor
Ruling n.	decision, decree
Ruminate vb.	muse, mediate, ponder, think, reflect
Rumor n.	gossip, hearsay
Rumple vb.	wrinkle, crumble n. wrinkle, crumple, crease
Run vb.	speed, hurry, hasten, go, flow n. sprint, dash, rush
Run away vb. phr.	escape, flee
Run down vb. phr.	hunt, seize, catch
Run into vb. phr.	crash, collide, encounter
Run out vb. phr.	dissipate
Run-of-the-mill adj.	ordinary, common
Rupture n.	split, true, disruption
Rural adj.	rustic, pastoral
Rush vb.	run, hasten, speed
Rustic adj.	rural, unpolished, uncouth
Ruthless adj.	pitiless, unrelenting, unrelenting, inhuman

S

Sable adj.	dark, dusky, somber, black
Scared adj.	hallowed, divine, consecrated
Safe adj.	protected, secure **n.** safety
Safeguard n.	protection
Sag vb.	droop, fail, weaken
Sagacious adj.	wise, judicious, rational, intelligent, astute
Sage adj.	wise, sagacious, rational, logical **n.** wiseman
Saintly adj.	devout, holy, good, moral, righteous
Sake n.	reason, purpose
Salary n.	wage, pay, compensation, payment
Salubrious adj.	healthy, healthful, wholesome
Salvage vb.	recover, save, rescue, receive
Salvation n.	deliverance
Same adj.	identical, equivalent
Sanction n.	permission, authorization **vb.** approve, refuge, shelter
Sanctuary n.	asylum, shelter
Sane adj.	rational, sound, normal, reasonable
Sanguine adj.	optimistic, blood-red, warm, lively, animated
Sanitary adj.	disinfected, hygienic
Sap vb.	exhaust, weaken, drain
Satanic adj.	diabolic, devilish, demonic
Satire n.	ridicule, sarcasm, irony
Satisfaction n.	pleasure, gratification, enjoyment
Satisfactory adj.	sufficient, okay

Satisfy vb.	meet, gratify, cheer, comfort
Saucy adj.	impudent, rude
Saunter vb.	amble, wander
Save vb.	free, liberate
Savoury adj.	relishing, piquant, nice, delicious
Say vb.	speak, utter, remark
Scamp n.	rascal, rouge
Scan vb.	glance at or over, study
Scarce adj.	rare, sparse, scanty, insufficient
Scathe vb.	injure, harm, waste, blast **n.** damage, injure
Scatter vb.	spread, sprinkle
Schism n.	division, split, disunion
Scholar n.	student, savant, wiseman
Scintillate vb.	sparkle, flash
Scold vb.	reprove, reprimand, censure
Score n.	record, tally, reckoning
Scourge n.	affliction, plague
Scowl vb. n.	glare, frown, glower, scramble
Scrap n.	part, fragment **vb.** junk, discard
Scrape vb.	scour, rub
Scream vb. n.	shriek, screech
Screech vb. n.	scream, shriek, yell
Scrimmage n.	skirmish, scuffle
Scrimp vb.	save, conserve, skimp
Scrub vb.	scour, wash, clean
Scrupulous adj.	critical, exacting, careful, fastidious
Scrutinize vb.	examine
Scurrilous adj.	outrageous, insulting, insolent

Scurry vb.	scramble, hasten, scamper
Scuttle vb.	sink, ditch, swamp
Seasoned adj.	experienced, veteran
Secede vb.	resign, quit
Secluded adj.	isolated, sheltered, hidden
Sedate adj.	calm, unruffled, serene, composed
Sediment n.	dregs, lees, residue
Sedition n.	insurrection, insurgence, riot, rising
Segment n.	section, division, part, portion
Segregate vb.	separate, ostracize
Sensible adj.	reasonable, commonsensical
Sensual adj.	erotic, sexual, lustful, carnal, lewd
Sentiment n.	feeling, attitude, tenderness, emotion
Sequence n.	order, series, arrangement
Sequester vb.	separate, set aside, remove, put aside
Serene adj.	peaceful, quiet
Session n.	meeting, sitting
Severe adj.	cruel, firm, unyielding
Sew vb.	stitch, mend
Shabby adj.	ragged
Shackle n.	fetter, manacle, hand cuff
Shade n.	shadow, gloom, dusk, tint, colour
Shaggy adj.	wooly, hairy, uncombed, unkempt
Shield n.	guard, defense, shelter
Shifty adj.	crafty, shrewd, cunning, tricky
Shirk vb.	avoid, evade, dodge
Shiver vb.	tremble, quiver, shudder, shake
Shovel n.	spade
Shriek vb. n.	scream, screech

Shrill adj.	sharp, piercing
Shrivel vb.	shrink, contract, dwindle, whither, decrease, parch, dry up, dry
Shudder vb. n.	shiver, tremble, shake, quiver
Shun vb.	evade, elude
Sibilant adj.	hissing, sibilous, buzzing
Sinewy adj.	muscular, wiry, vigorous
Siren n.	mermaid, tempter, fascinating
Skeptical adj.	doubting, incredulous
Skimpy adj.	meager, scanty
Slapdash adv. collaq.	haphazard, without, forethought
Slim adj.	slender, thin, slight, small
Slipshod adj.	careless, sloppy
Slope vb.	incline, slant
Slumber n. vb.	sleep, rest, repose
Slump n.	decline, descent, depression
Smash vb.	break, crash, crush, demolish
Smattering n.	slight or superficial
Smear vb.	rub, spread, libel, defame
Smother vb.	stifle, asphyxiate, suffocate
Sneak vb.	slink, skulk, steal
Snicker vb.	titter, giggle
Snub vb.	rebuke
Sojourn n.	stay, lodge, rest, abode
Solicit vb.	request, seek, pray
Solicitous adj.	concerned
Solicitude n.	anxiety, care
Solitary adj.	isolated, deserted, sole, only, single

Somnolent adj.	sleepy, dozy
Sonorous adj.	high-sounding, ringing, full-toned
Soothe vb.	calm, pacify
Sophist n.	fallacious, artful
Sotto voce adj.	softly, in a low
Souvenir n. fr.	reminder, keepsake, remembrance
Sparing adj.	frugal, thrifty, parsimonious
Sparse adj.	scattered, spread here and there
Spasm n.	twitch, sudden, cramp
Species n.	class, sort, kind
Specific adj.	definite, particular
Specimen n.	sample, example, model type
Specious adj.	plausible, apparently
Speck n.	bit, sport, mite
Specter n.	apparition, ghost, phantom, goblin
Spellbound adj.	entranced, fascinated, mesmerised
Spendthrift n.	squandered, profligate
Spirited adj.	animated, active, lively, energetic, vivacious
Splay adj.	wide, broad, spreading, turned out
Splendour n.	magnificence
Sporting adj.	fair, considerate, sportsmanlike
Spotty adj.	uneven, inconsistent, erratic, irregular
Spout vb.	squirt, spurt
Spring n.	twig, shot, spray, youth, lad
Sprightly adj.	spry, nimble, vivacious
Sprite n.	fairy, fay, pixy
Spry adj.	lively, nimble, quick

Squabble vb.	quarrel, argue, bicker, row
Squat vb.	sit close **adj.** couching
Stable adj.	steady, firm, steadfast, solid
Stagger vb.	sway, totter, reel, falter, vary
Staid adj.	sober, grave, steady, serious, composed
Stain n.	spot, blemish
Stake n.	post, stick, pole, wager, bet, interest
Stalk vb.	follow, dog, shadow
Stall vb.	stop, hesitate, postpone, delay
Stamina n.	strength, vigour, force, stoutness
Staple adj.	principle, main, chief
Startle vb.	surprise, agitate, alarm
Statuesque adj.	stately, majestic, regal, dignified
Stature n.	height, tallness
Stead n.	place
Steal vb.	pilfer, rob embezzle
Stench n.	stink, fetor
Stern adj.	strict, severe, harsh, hard, rigid
Stickler n.	perfectionist, disciplinarian
Stigma n.	mark, blemish
Stimulant adj.	stimulating, provocative
Stipulate vb.	demand, require
Stoop vb.	bend, lean, bow
Stout adj.	fat, obese, heavy, portly, sturdy
Straightforward adj.	direct, forthright, candid
Strainer n.	sieve
Strait n.	channel, passage, distress

Straitlaced adj.	strict, formal
Stratagem n.	ruse, subterfuge, wile, trick
Strategy n.	management, approach
Stenuous adj.	energetic, active
Strife n.	conflict, disagreement, difference
Stringent adj.	binding, strict, rigid
Stroll vb. n.	walk, amble
Stultify vb.	make foolish, foolish, besot
Stupendous adj.	astonishing, surprising, amazing
Stupor n.	lethargy, narcosis, numbness, coma
Sturdy adj.	rugged, well-built
Subdue vb.	defeat, conquer, beat
Subside vb.	sink, lower, diminish
Subsidise vb.	supply with a subsidy, aid, finance
Subsidy n.	grant, support, aid
Substantial adj.	considerable, large, sizable, real, actual
Subtle adj.	indirect, suggestive
Succor vb.	aid, assist, help, nurse, comfort
Succulent adj.	juicy, lush, full of juice, nutritive
Succumb vb.	yield, submit, surrender
Suffix n.	ending
Suffrage n.	vote, voice, ballot, attestation, testimonial
Suffuse vb.	overspread, cover, bathe
Sultry adj.	hot, oppressive, stifling
Sundry adj.	various
Supervene vb.	accessory, follow upon
Supplement n.	addition, complement, extension

Suppress vb.	overpower
Surfeit vb.	satiate, glut, gorge
Surge vb.	swell, heave, grow
Surely adj.	unfriendly, hostile
Surpass vb.	exceed, pass, excel
Susceptible adj.	impressible, receptive
Swamp n.	bog, quagmire, marsh, morass
Sway vb.	wave, bend, influence, persuade
Swindle vb.	cheat, bilk, cozen, trick, deceive
Swindler n.	rogue, knave, embezzler
Sycophant n.	parasite, wheedler, cringer
Sylvan adj.	forest-like n. satyr, faun
Symphony n.	consonance, music, concert
Synonym n.	equivalent word, word of nearly the same meaning

T

Taboo adj.	prohibited, banned, forbidden, inviolable
Tacit adj.	implied, understood, silent, unspoken
Taciturn adj.	silent, reserved, close, reticent
Tackle n.	equipment
Act n.	judgment, diplomacy, prudence
Tactics n. pl.	strategy, plan
Taint vb.	corrupt, tarnish
Take after vb. phr.	resemble

Tally vb.	match, agree
Tame adj.	domesticated, docile
Tangle vb.	knot, twist
Tantalise vb.	tempt, tease
Tardy adj.	late, unpunctual, slow
Tarnish vb.	soil, stain, sully, smudge, blemish
Tart adj.	acid, sour, sharp
Taste vb.	savor n. flavor, savor, appreciation, discernment
Tasteless adj.	insipid, unpalatable, unrefined
Tallte vb.	reveal, blab
Tautology n.	repetition, reiteration, verbosity
Tawdry adj.	showy, gaudy
Tawny adj.	yellowish, dull yellow
Techy adj.	peevish, tretful
Tedious adj.	tiring, tiresome
Teem vb.	swarm, abound
Temerity n.	recklessness, rash, heedlessness, hastiness, audacity
Temporize vb.	comply with, occasions, hedge
Tenacious adj.	determined, persistent, unchanging, firmness
Tender adj.	delicate, soft, fragile, loving, gentle, affectionate
Tepid adj.	lukewarm, slightly
Terse adj.	concise, brief, short, compact, laconic
Test n.	trial, examination

Testify vb.	warrant, depose
Thaw vb.	melt, liquefy, dissolve
Thesaurus n.	dictionary, glossary, repository, treasure
Thoroughbred adj.	well-versed, trained, proficient, well-educated
Thoroughfare n.	street, highway, avenue, boulevard
Thrash vb.	beat, whip, defeat
Thrifty adj.	frugal, sparing, economical
Throe n.	fit, paroxysm, spam, anguish, pang
Throng n.	crowd, multitude, swarm, mass, horde
Thrust vb.	push, shove, force
Thwart vb.	frustrate, obstruct, stop
Tiding n. pl.	news, information, word, report
Tiff n.	squabble, quarrel, argument
Timbre n.	quality (of tone), clang, tone, colour
Tinge vb. n.	tint, colour, dye
Tinker vb.	putter, potter, fiddle
Tint b. vb.	tinge, colour, dye, stain
Toil vb.	work, labour, sweat
Token n.	sign, mark, sample
Tranquility n.	quiet, quietness, stillness, quietude
Transform vb.	change
Transparent adj.	clear, limpid, clear, obvious
Transpire vb.	pass off in vapor, be disclosed, become known
Transude vb.	exude, ooze, percolate

Trashy adj.	worthless, insignificant, slight
Treachery n.	betrayal, disloyalty
Tremendous adj.	huge, enormous, gigantic
Trench n.	ditch, gully, moat, gorge, gulch
Trenchant adj.	cutting, incisive, severe
Trepidation n.	shaking, trembling, quaking, quivering
Trespasser n.	intruder, invader, encroacher
Trice n.	moment, instant, jiffy, flash
Trifling adj.	unimportant, trivial, petty, insignificant
Trimmings n.	ornaments, trappings, dress, gear
Trite adj.	stale, beaten, hackneyed, worn out, stereotyped
Trivial adj.	trifling, unimportant, petty, insignificant
Troglodyte n.	wretch, outcast
Troll vb.	send about
Truant n.	idler, shirk, loiter, idling
Truce n.	armistice, suspension, respite, lull, recess
Truism n.	axiom, self-evident
Truneate vb.	lop, maim, cut off, dock
Tryst n.	appointment, rendezvous
Tumult n.	to-do, disturbance, commotion
Twilight n.	dusk, nightfall
Twinge n.	pang, pain, smart

U

Ubiquitous adj.	omnipresent, universally present
Ugly adj.	evil
Ultimatum n.	final condition, final proposition
Ululation n.	howling, wailing, howl, cry, crying, yelp, bellowing, hoot
Umbrage n.	shade, shadow, offence, resentment, pique, grudge, dudgeon
Unadulterated adj.	unmixed, undiluted, neat, genuine, pure, clear, real, true, sincere, honest
Unanimity n.	agreement, unity, accord
Unanimous adj.	concordant, agreeing, united, harmonious, likeminded
Unassuming adj.	modest, humble, retiring
Unbridled adj.	unrestrained, licentious, licensed, lax, violent, uncontrolled
Uncanny adj.	remarkable, amazing, extraordinary
Uncouth adj.	vulgar, rude, ill-mannered
Unruffled adj.	smooth, unperturbed, calm, serene, cool
Unscathed adj.	uninjured, unharmed
Untidy adj.	sloopy, messy, slovenly, disorderly
Usher n. vb.	guide, introduce, forerun, herald

V

Vacuum n.	avoid, empty space, vacuity
Vague adj.	uncertain, indefinite, unsure, obscure

Valiant adj.	brave, bold, courageous, heroic, intrepid, dauntless, unafraid, fearless
Valor n.	bravery, boldness, courage, intrepidity, heroism, fearlessness
Variable adj.	changeable, shifting, unsteady
Vaudeville n. fr.	ballad, street, song, light
Vault n.	tomb, sepulcher, crypt, grave, catacomb, safe, safety-deposit box
Vengeance n.	revenge, retaliation
Venom n.	poison, toxin, spite, bitterness, hate
Venture n.	attempt, risk, chance, test **vb.** risk, dare, gamble, hazard
Verbose adj.	wordy, prolix, diffuse, talkative, loquacious
Verdant adj.	green, fresh
Verdict n.	decision, judgment, opinion, finding
Verge n.	edge, rim, lip, margin, brim, brink
Versatile adj.	changeable, variable, mobile, capricious, kaleidoscopic
Veto n.	denial, refusal **vb.** deny, refuse, negate, prohibit, forbid
Vicinity n.	neighborhood, area
Vicissitude n.	alteration, interchange, regular, change, mutual, succession
Victuals n. pl.	food, meat, sustenance, provisions, viands, eatables, comestibles
Vigorous adj.	energetic, strong, active, forceful powerful

Vindicate vb.	justify, defend, uphold, assert, maintain, support, stand by, advocate right, avenge
Virtue n.	goodness, morality, righteousness, honour, merit, quality, advantage
Virtuous adj.	moral, upright, upstanding, ethical
Virtuoso n.	connoisseur, expert, skilled person master
Vivacious adj.	animated, lively, spirited, sprightly
Vocation n.	career, profession occupation calling, employment
Vogue n.	fashion, mode, style, usage, custom, practice
Volant adj.	flying, current, mumble, rapid, quick, light, active
Vouchsafe vb.	concede, grant, accord, allow, deign to grant, condescend, yield, stoop, oath
Vulnerable adj.	defenseless, unguarded, unprotected
Vulpine adj.	cunning, crafty, artful, sly, wily, foxy, of a fox
Vulturine adj.	rapacious, ravenous

W

Wage vb.	carry on, pursue, conduct, make
Wail vb.	moan, cry, mourn, bewail, lament **n.** moan, cry
Wallow vb.	flounder, roll, toss, welter, tumble, grovel, live in filth

Warden n.	guardian, custodian, keeper, guard, jailer, turnkey
Wary adj.	cautious, careful, needful, prudent
Ways and means n. pl.	methods, resources, facilities
Weakling n.	sissy, milquetoast, milksop, namby-pamby
Wealth n.	riches, fortune, property, means, money, quantity, abundance, profession
Weighty adj.	significant, important, crucial
Wharf n.	dock, pier
Wheedle vb.	cajole, coax, persuade
Whelp n.	cub, young, beast, puppy, pup, young dog
Whimsical adj.	strange, fanciful, capricious, notional, erratic, queer, quaint
Wield vb.	brandish, handle, manage, use, make use of
Wilt vb.	droop, sag, weaken
Wit n.	intelligence, understanding, wisdom, humor, wittiness, drollery, humourist, comedian, wag
Wrangle vb.	quarrel, bicker, spar, spat, jangle, squabble
Wrench n. vb.	twist, jerk, tug
Wring vb.	extract, twist
Writhe vb.	squirm, twist

X

Xanthous adj.	fair, blond, light, complexioned, fair-complexioned, fair-haired, blond-haired, yellow-haired

Y

Yacht n.	boat, pleasure craft, sailboat, cruiser
Yarn n.	thread, fiber, tale, story, anecdote
Yawn vb.	gape, gape, open, open-wide, threaten to engulf
Yearn vb.	desire, want, crave, long for, covet

Z

Zany n.	buffoon, clown, jester, droll, punch
Zeal n.	eagerness, enthusiasm, fervor, passion, devotion
Zealous adj.	ardent, eager, enthusiastic
Zenith n.	top, acme, pinnacle, summit, apex
Zephyr n.	west wind, gentle, mild or soft breeze, light wind
Zest n.	spice, relish, tang, gusto, enjoyment, thrill
Zip n.	energy, vigour, vitality, vim

www.ingramcontent.com/pod-product-compliance
Lightning Source LLC
Chambersburg PA
CBHW020802160426
43192CB00006B/412